IS THIS AMERICA?

D1366589

THE KATRINA BOOKSHELF

Kai Erikson, Series Editor

In 2005 Hurricane Katrina crashed into the Gulf Coast and precipitated the flooding of New Orleans. It was a towering catastrophe by any standard. Some 1,800 persons were killed outright. More than a million were forced to relocate, many for the remainder of their lives. A city of five hundred thousand was nearly emptied of life. The storm stripped away the surface of our social structure and showed us what lies beneath—a grim picture of race, class, and gender in these United States.

It is crucial to get this story straight so that we may learn from it and be ready for that stark inevitability, *the next time*. When seen through a social science lens, Katrina informs us of the real human costs of a disaster and helps prepare us for the events that we know are lurking just over the horizon. The Katrina Bookshelf is the result of a national effort to bring experts together in a collaborative program of research on the human costs of the disaster. The program was supported by the Ford, Gates, MacArthur, Rockefeller, and Russell Sage Foundations and sponsored by the Social Science Research Council. This is the most comprehensive social science coverage of a disaster to be found anywhere in the literature. It is also a deeply human story.

IS THIS AMERICA?

KATRINA AS CULTURAL TRAUMA

RON EYERMAN

University of Texas Press

AUSTIN

Requests for permission to reproduce material from this work should be sent to:
Permissions
University of Texas Press
P.O. Box 7819
Austin, TX 78713-7819
http://utpress.utexas.edu/index.php/rp-form

♾ The paper used in this book meets the minimum requirements of
ANSI/NISO Z39.48-1992 (R1997) (Permanence of Paper).

LIBRARY OF CONGRESS CATALOGING-IN-PUBLICATION DATA

Eyerman, Ron, author.
Is this America? : Katrina as cultural trauma / Ron Eyerman. — First edition.
pages cm — (The Katrina bookshelf)
Includes bibliographical references and index.
ISBN 978-1-4773-0368-9 (cloth : alk. paper)
ISBN 978-1-4773-0547-8 (pbk. : alk. paper)
ISBN 978-1-4773-0746-5 (library e-book)
ISBN 978-1-4773-0747-2 (nonlibrary e-book)
1. Hurricane Katrina, 2005—Social aspects. 2. Refugees—Louisiana—
New Orleans—Social conditions. 3. Disaster victims—United States—Social
conditions. 4. Social problems—Psychological aspects. 5. Psychic trauma—
Social aspects—Louisiana—New Orleans. 6. Hurricane Katrina, 2005—
Press coverage. I. Title. II. Series: Katrina bookshelf.
HV636 2005 .N4 E94 2015
976'.044—dc23   2014049381

doi:10.7560/303689

For Kai Erikson

CONTENTS

ACKNOWLEDGMENTS   ix

1. Breaking the Covenant   1

2. Print Media   20

3. Arts and Popular Culture   52

4. Television Coverage   92

Conclusion   120

NOTES   149

BIBLIOGRAPHY   157

ABOUT THE AUTHOR AND SERIES EDITOR   165

INDEX   167

ACKNOWLEDGMENTS

It was Kai Erikson who first proposed that I write this book. Kai headed a group of researchers with partial funding from the Social Science Research Council to compile a series of books about the impact of Hurricane Katrina. The group was well established by the time I met them for the first time in New Orleans in October 2011, six years after that terrible disaster we were meant to study. I think they were a little suspicious of me, the newcomer, wondering about my stance toward our common subject. While they had all been on the ground gathering data for several years, here I was parachuting in, a cultural sociologist no less, with seemingly fixed ideas about the "meaning" of Katrina. My first attempts at specificity were not particularly well received; I recall some very skeptical comments as we sat around the conference table in our faux French hotel in the business district. Over the past two years I have exchanged ideas and manuscript pages with these colleagues and hopefully gained some of their trust. They are the first audience I had in mind as I wrote this book.

Kai Erikson has read every word of my several draft manuscripts, seeing to it that I eliminated many superfluous thoughts. Lori Peek read and commented on several chapters and has been very generous in her support. Steve Kroll-Smith, Shirley Laska, and others in the group have also provided insightful comments. Nadya Jaworsky's editing skills were a significant factor in my first drafts, and her knowledge of cultural sociology added to my confidence as I read her substantial comments. Alison Gerber helped with the final editing and in preparing the manuscript for publication. Joseph Klett gathered the television data and Karianne Esseveld did extensive research on music and popular culture. Research librarians at the Yale, Tulane, and City of New Orleans libraries helped me find the necessary materials. Ben Alexander-Bloch helped arrange interviews at the *Times-Picayune*, and Ed and Hilary Moise provided warm accommodations and friendship during my stay in New Orleans. We shared their gourmet food and love of the city. Johanna Esseveld made this trip even more warm and successful.

My colleagues at the Yale Center for Cultural Sociology, especially my codirectors Jeffrey Alexander and Philip Smith, were generous in their comments and support for this research. I thank them and all those who participated in our workshops for their insights. Nadine Amalfi worked very hard to get my manuscript looking like a book, spending hours compiling data and hounding publishers and artists for permission to cite their work. Thank you all!

IS THIS AMERICA?

BREAKING THE COVENANT

*"The people I swore I'd serve and protect—they're floating.
They're dead. I didn't sign up for this . . . These are American
citizens dying. This is not Burundi. These are not Hutus and Tutsis,
or whatever, you know? They are American citizens."*

NEW ORLEANS POLICE OFFICER QUOTED IN COOPER,
DISPATCHES FROM THE EDGE, 2006

*"They came already here—the exile and the stranger, brave
but frightened—to find a place where a man could be his own man.
They made a covenant with this land. Conceived in justice, written
in liberty, bound in union, it was meant one day to inspire the
hopes of all mankind; and it binds us still."*

LYNDON BAINES JOHNSON

These fine words uttered by Lyndon Johnson during his inaugural address
in January 1965 recall a long rhetorical tradition embedded in what sociologist Robert Bellah has called America's civil religion.[1] President Johnson and many American leaders before and after have filled their public
addresses with religious sentiment that resonates with myths defining the
self-understanding of the American nation. America is a nation formed
"under God" with a mission to do good in the world. It is a country of "almost chosen people," to use Abraham Lincoln's famous phrase, who have
a covenant, a sacred agreement. In Bellah's estimation, the covenant has
been broken a number of times in the nation's history, the Civil War being
perhaps the most obvious breach and the Vietnam War another. To these
one could add the Watergate scandal and, more abstractly, but also much
more significantly, the failure of a wealthy nation to alleviate poverty and
racism—the failure to even notice what Michael Harrington once called

The Other America. That covenant was broken yet again during Hurricane Katrina, when that other America was so dramatically and tragically exposed to full public view.[2]

In one of the peculiarities of American political culture, elected officials and those appointed to public office, including police and judicial authorities, are literally sworn in, a process known as administering an "oath of office." This reflects the direct influence of the covenant referred to by Lyndon Johnson. In front of legal witnesses, appointed authorities raise their right hands while placing their left on a sacred text (almost exclusively the Bible) and pledge to uphold the laws of the land "so help me God." I believe this to be unusual if not unique in modern society. While such rituals may seem empty gestures, sociological studies argue to the contrary that they carry deep-seated meaning and moral force for those who perform them. The very idea of an office and the practice of being sworn in carry both legal and moral force. Failure to fulfill one's obligation can result in formal punishment and public shaming: one can be formally relieved of one's duties, dishonorably discharged. In many parts of the world such actions are restricted to military affairs, but in the United States, which takes pride in the local, participatory nature of its democratic traditions, these sentiments and practices permeate the entire system of government, from the presidency to the small-town police officer, as the previous quotation reveals.

During and after Katrina, the relief and rescue efforts organized by local, state, and federal authorities—the government of the United States, from the top down—failed its people. Even before Hurricane Katrina made landfall in the coastal regions of Louisiana and Mississippi, those entrusted to carry out the promises of the covenant had failed in their duty to adequately protect the residents of the Gulf. In a long history of mismanagement, regional political leaders had diverted monies meant to maintain the fragile levee system that protected rural and urban areas from flooding.[3] At the same time, the wetlands that served as a natural buffer against wind and water were being systematically destroyed by commercial interests, with the acknowledgment and consent of elected political officials. All of this helped turn a natural force into a social disaster.

Then, as the terrible winds began to subside and as the floodwaters rushed through rural and urban areas, many of those same officials failed miserably in their sworn duty to protect the people in their charge. In New Orleans, the place with the most concentrated population and thus the most visible to mass media, there was a clear lack of leadership in the face of oncoming disaster. A writer for the *Times-Picayune* stated, "The assumption that poor people would be trapped was met with inaction, when it should have been met with determination to save as many as possible."[4] The city's mayor, Ray Nagin, became a symbol of incompetence and uncaring. According to historian Douglas Brinkley, Nagin "implemented no comprehensive plan to evacuate vulnerable people" and "had little interest in the 112,000 adult New Orleanians who didn't own cars. They were, in his mindset, a secondary concern."[5] Rather than offering public assistance, "Nagin urged those people to seek rides with friends, family, neighbors, and church members."[6] At the time of this writing, Nagin is under indictment for public corruption. For its part, the city's police force, 15 percent of whom abandoned their posts and fled, was seen by many as a brutal gang of marauders patrolling in search of loot and creating mayhem instead of preventing it. "High-tailing NOPD officers had lost track of rules and regulations; many just drove their patrol cars straight out of the bowl to Texas. A few of those who stayed in New Orleans were 'outlaw' cops, not accountable to anybody—desperados looking for a quick score like a Panasonic plasma TV or a Sony CD player."[7] Like former mayor Nagin, the New Orleans police department is currently being investigated by federal authorities.

As one went up the chain of command, from the city's police leadership to state and federal authorities, the failure seemed only to intensify. The federal authorities blamed state and local officials for the slow response. Louisiana governor Kathleen Blanco was the target of the harshest criticism, and the favor was returned in kind by federal authorities. The national authority charged with emergency preparedness and response, the Federal Emergency Management Agency (FEMA), was the most visible failure, though its actions were actually limited by the Department of Homeland Security, higher up the chain. FEMA's director, Michael Brown, became the face of government mismanagement and neglect. With people dying on the flooded streets, trapped in attics, and stranded on rooftops and highway overpasses, FEMA hesitated to take action. "When FEMA finally did show up, everybody was angry because all they had was a website and a flyer," said Mark Pryor, a senator from Arkansas, in testimony given to a congressional investigating committee.

Finally, the president, the person in charge of overseeing the covenant, appeared in public and in photographs in ways that suggested serene passivity with regard to the suffering of citizens in the region. In what became an iconic media image, George W. Bush was shown flying over the Gulf and praising his old friend, FEMA director Brown, whom he referred to as "Brownie," for "doing a heck of a job." As the holder of the nation's highest office and as the person formally responsible for the Katrina rescue efforts, President Bush became a symbolic figure as much as an active participant in the public debates that followed in the aftermath of the storm. His failure was America's failure.

THE STORM TAKES FORM

Tropical Storm Katrina was baptized on Wednesday morning, August 24, 2005, when its winds reached 40 miles an hour about 230 miles east of Miami. It was the eleventh storm of the season. The next day it became Hurricane Katrina as its winds measured 75 miles an hour, which qualified it as a Category 1 hurricane according to the Saffir-Simpson scale, the official storm measure. At this time it lay off the Florida coast just east of Fort Lauderdale, ready to come ashore. By 7:00 p.m. that day, Thursday, August 25, two people had died from falling trees. By the next day the winds had subsided and Katrina was downgraded back to a tropical storm. As it moved westward into the Gulf along the Florida panhandle, the winds strengthened once again and it was recategorized as a hurricane. By 11:30 a.m. on Friday, August 26, the National Hurricane Center reported that Katrina was rapidly intensifying in strength and its winds had increased to over 100 miles an hour. With this news, the governors of Mississippi and Louisiana declared a state of emergency, and by 11:00 p.m. the National Hurricane Center was predicting a major hurricane in the Gulf region. By 5:00 a.m. on Saturday, August 27, Katrina recorded winds of 115 miles an hour, making it a Category 3 hurricane. By Sunday it became a Category 4, with winds of over 145 miles an hour, as it moved north toward the Mississippi Delta. At 11:00 a.m. it reached Category 5 status, the highest designation, with winds reaching 175 miles. Just prior to that, at 9:30 a.m., New Orleans mayor Ray Nagin issued a mandatory evacuation order for the entire city. "We are facing the storm most of us have feared. This is going to be an unprecedented event," he declared.[8]

All of these phrases—tropical storm, hurricane, and the various numbered categories—have meaning for those who hear and say them. For the authorities, these terms are measurements, categories of severity based on a calculation of wind speed and potential damage. For ordinary citizens, especially those living on the Gulf coast, they are terms that call to mind past experiences with similarly named phenomena. This is also true of the authorities taking the measurements and making the calculations, where categories of severity recall earlier exemplars. Hurricane Katrina was measured against and compared to previous hurricanes as a means of making clear the potential damage that could come from wind and water. According to the U.S. Department of Commerce and the National Weather Service, "Experience shows that the use of short, distinctive given names in written as well as spoken communications is quicker and less subject to error than the older more cumbersome latitude-longitude identification methods . . . The use of easily remembered names greatly reduces confusion when two or more tropical storms occur at the same time" (http://aoml.noaa.gov /general/lib/reason.html).

There is more than efficient communication involved in the naming of hurricanes, however; names call forth images and evoke vivid memories in ways that numbers do not. This is especially true in regard to popular memory. Citizens of New Orleans and the wider Gulf region had a rich frame of reference to draw upon as they interpreted the authoritative pronouncements about the oncoming storm. Their memories of past storms affected the way they understood the words and how they planned to react to them. Katrina brought forth images of previous hurricanes such as Betsy from 1963 and Camille from 1969. As Katrina approached, a local sheriff told CNN, "You're now looking at a Category 5. You're looking at a storm that is as strong as Camille was, but bigger than Betsy was size-wise."[9]

Such memories not only helped put the coming threat in perspective but also provided both those in authority and average citizens with a framework for deciding a proper course of action. Like the professionals watching the colorful storm images moving across their computer screens, residents judged the potential danger not only by tracking the storm but also by considering what they had experienced or heard about the past. In the Gulf region, such recollections often had racial and class dimensions drawn from a rich reservoir of stories stretching back as far as the 1927 Mississippi River flood, when levees were dynamited and African American neighborhoods were flooded in a desperate effort to save other parts of the city. In 2005, African American residents of New Orleans believed this would happen again in order to save the more affluent and whiter parts of the city. In Katrina's aftermath one black resident, Dyan French, known locally as "Mamma D," testified before the House Select Committee that this in fact had occurred. "I was on my front porch. I have witnesses that they bombed the walls of the levee, boom, boom! Mister, I'll never forget it."[10]

Hurricane Katrina was no ordinary disaster. In terms of official recorded deaths (1,836), it was the third highest in U.S. history. It was the costliest disaster on record, causing somewhere between $80 and 120 billion in losses. Katrina was remarkable not only because of its devastation, but also because of how it was experienced, understood, and interpreted. It was described as unprecedented and unexpected, a natural disaster followed by a monumental governmental failure that brought shame to a great nation. The phrase "Hurricane Katrina" now carries an emotionally charged and contentious range of connotations. For many it has come to symbolize an American tragedy. The storm was a traumatic occurrence, a shocking incident that threatened established routines of understanding and action. As its story unfolded through the mass media, Katrina became an event of great significance not only for those who directly suffered its wrath, but, at least for a time, for the rest of the nation as well.

From this perspective, Katrina was not only a devastating hurricane that demolished homes and livelihoods in the Gulf region but also a social disaster that destroyed communities and tore at the threads of collective identity. The hurricane evoked cultural trauma, a profound public reflection on the meaning of this devastation that reached into the very foundational narratives and myths which ground the nation itself. In the public debate that followed in its aftermath, a wide range of voices and images were invoked to clarify what happened, to name who was responsible, to identify the victims, and to decide what was to be done. The discussion took place in a number of forums, most notably the mass media and the political arena, but also in various realms of the arts and popular culture. This book will map, trace, and analyze the public discourse by highlighting the narratives that emerged and competed to tell the story of Katrina. It will draw conclusions with regard to the theory of cultural trauma, but even more significantly, it will ponder how Katrina has affected the idea of America itself, its collective identity and memory.

THE LEVELS OF TRAUMA

There are common medical, psychological, and social psychological applications of the term "trauma." Kai Erikson proposes that traumatic wounds are collective and social as well as individual, and that trauma can create as well as destroy communality.[11] He writes, "Trauma has both centripetal and centrifugal tendencies. It draws one away from the center of group space while at the same time drawing one back."[12]

As I use the term, "cultural" trauma has much in common with this conception. I too view shocking incidents as the basis of collective trauma, but I do not believe that shocking incidents—what I would call traumatic occurrences—in themselves cause cultural trauma. All traumas may be social, but not all become the basis for an understanding of an incident or occurrence as traumatic. Nor do all such incidents lead to intense public debate on their meaning. In my view, there is no necessary, causal relation between a traumatic incident, where individuals or collectivities suffer terribly, and a cultural trauma. There are several layers of meaning and significant actors that mediate between a shocking occurrence and a cultural trauma. Hurricane Katrina was traumatic in Kai Erikson's sense of the term; it was a shocking incident that caused great pain and suffering. But the hurricane in itself did not cause a cultural trauma; what did was the failure of those charged with collective responsibility, the upholders of the covenant, to act accordingly. It was this failure and all the deep-seated cleavages it exposed that catalyzed a great public debate in which the foundations of collective identity were brought up for reflection. It was a debate that raised the question, "Is this America?"

From the previous discussion, one can distinguish three categories of trauma: individual, collective, and cultural. Individual trauma is well documented and the term has an everyday as well as a professional usage. Psychologists since the late nineteenth century have applied the term to describe the effects of accidents and childhood sexual abuse; it continues to be used today, some would argue to excess, in relation to the effects of war, extreme poverty, and violent crime. As has been well documented by other books in this Katrina Shelf series, there can be no doubt as to the individual trauma found in Katrina's aftermath. The number of people left devastated and abandoned on rooftops and attics, in old-age homes or at the Superdome without proper provision, is evidence enough. There is also plenty of evidence of group or collective trauma, of families broken apart, neighborhoods destroyed, and whole communities uprooted. These two types of trauma may also be thought of as reinforcing one another, making the shock and sense of loss even greater. Such was the case in the tightly knit neighborhoods of New Orleans, in the Mississippi Delta, and in the communities along the Gulf coast, where personal loss was intimately tied to losses suffered by neighbors. The cumulative impact would only intensify the trauma where a sense of belonging, a collective identity, was shattered along with individual identity. Individual and collective traumas are thus bound up with one another and are mutually reinforcing, but cultural trauma as I use it here is a dimension apart and refers to more abstract and mediated notions of racial and national identity such as is encapsulated in the idea of a national covenant. Cultural trauma is most often connected to a traumatic incident and thus to individual and collective trauma, but its occurrence is contingent on a number of factors, as will be elaborated later in this book. One can conceive of situations where there is great individual and collective trauma but no cultural trauma: a tornado destroying a small town, an earthquake uprooting a village, or a political assassination affecting groups and institutions but not threatening collective identity in a fundamental way.

Cultural traumas are public articulations of collective pain and suffering that require representation through word, sound, and image as well as interested parties to construct and communicate them. These take form as narratives that create and cultivate a unified experience for disparate individuals. Such narration turns the individual experience of trauma into a coherent meaning framework, a story, helping traumatized individuals to make better sense of what has happened to them. The mass media and popular culture are important mechanisms in making this happen, as will be discussed in the coming chapters.

NARRATING TRAUMA

It was not by chance that in the midst of the storm, a local radio host helped narrate what was happening as it occurred. Journalists are often the first to offer a general framework in which to insert and make sense out of the individual experience of shock and disaster. As discussed previously, the concept "hurricane" is itself a narrative device that not only names a phenomenon but in so doing places it in relation to others. This situational and relational understanding influences how one reacts to ongoing occurrences. Once the name is applied and accepted, all the extraordinary things that are occurring can be understood with reference to it, including the pain and suffering of individuals. This associative reference occurs at several levels; through it, those directly affected make sense of what is happening in their immediate surroundings, while those more distant use the narrative frame to make sense of the images and stories they encounter in the mass media.

A cultural trauma is a publicly articulated response to a tear in the social fabric, when the foundations of an established collective identity are shaken and in need of a revised narrative. The process of cultural trauma as expressed in public debate can be understood as a meaning struggle, where individual and collective actors attempt to define the situation and impose a particular meaning on it. How contested, deep, and widespread was this debate about Katrina's meaning? How far did it reach into the collective foundations of the American nation? These are the questions this book will address. Was it deep and widespread enough to call it a national trauma? Arthur Neal has written about historic events that in his estimation caused "national trauma" in the United States.[13] His list includes the Great Depression, the assassinations of John F. Kennedy and Martin Luther King, and the Watergate scandal, among others. Neal defines a national trauma as an experience collectively felt, which "has enduring effects . . . in collective consciousness" and evokes images of living in a dangerous world in which "the borders and boundaries between order and chaos, between the sacred and the profane, between good and evil, between life and death become fragile." Like Kai Erikson, Neal connects a collective trauma to a precipitating event that evokes a feeling of crisis. A collective trauma becomes a national trauma when an entire nation is affected; it is the scope of the crisis that matters here. While I acknowledge a debt to Neal and a similarity between what he calls a national trauma and what I term a cultural trauma, there are significant differences. For one, I view trauma through the lens of cultural sociology as a social construction, a highly contingent process where several narratives compete and where the outcome is not simply a function of the event itself, no matter how forceful that might be. I prefer to speak of an incident or an occurrence rather than an event. In my view, events are themselves constructions; they must be made. No incident in itself causes a national trauma. There is usually some powerful occurrence that precipitates the process leading to cultural trauma, but no incident, no matter how powerful, creates or causes cultural trauma. As Neil Smelser put it, cultural traumas are made, not born. Making a cultural trauma is a process that involves actors or agents, what I will call carrier groups, who for various reasons take on the task of constructing a trauma narrative. One example of such a carrier group is journalists, working through mass media, who construct stories out of an incident, as will be elaborated below and throughout this book.

Cultural traumas are not things, but processes of meaning-making and attribution, contentious contests in which various individuals and groups struggle not only to define a situation but also to manage and control it. That is, they struggle to push collective understanding in particular directions. This attempt at management and control occurs simultaneously to an incident, as it unfolds, and also after the fact. There are two sides to a cultural trauma: an emotional experience and an interpretative reaction. Shocks arouse emotion by breaking everyday routines (behaviors as well as cognitive frameworks) and as such demand interpretation, opening a discursive field of interpretative opportunity where well-placed individuals can play a determinate role in making sense out of what has occurred. In modern societies, access to mass media is significant in this interpretative meaning-making process. They offer what seem like unmediated, firsthand accounts, which will have an impact on the understandings of others. These firsthand accounts, however, are selected and organized through prearranged scripts, remnants of previous experience and seemingly similar incidents, just as they are for ordinary citizens. Media scripts are more formalized, however; they have been not only molded by experience but also tried and tested for impact and effect. The news media tend to dramatize and personalize narratives, as well as to categorize them. The polarity between perpetrator and victim is one characteristic that distinguishes cultural trauma as a discursive process, and these are categories readily applied in mass-mediated accounts. These media accounts and the categories they apply are crucial factors in the articulation and construction of social traumas. How an unfolding incident is framed and coded and how it is valued are significant determinants in how it will be received and evaluated by others.

Yet cultural traumas are more than a struggle between competing actors to define a situation, to distinguish perpetrator and victim, and to identify the nature of the pain. That would limit the process to instrumental or strategic interaction. Cultural traumas are responses to deeply felt emotions that are publicly expressed and represented in this very same process, which implies an expressive and communicative aspect that makes claims to authenticity and sincerity. Anything connected to identity is bound up with powerful emotions. There are deeply rooted emotions and scripted identities to be drawn upon in such situations. I think here of racial, ethnic, or national identities that may lie under the surface but that can be mobilized in the face of a shocking occurrence. Such was clearly the case with Katrina. Mediated accounts must somehow fit with such deeply felt emotions—individual and collective trauma—as they shape and form how cultural traumas are understood. People are suffering and in shock, which scripted narrative frames applied through the mass media must acknowledge while they attempt to provide an understanding of how and why an incident happened.

A question that often emerges after a shocking incident and in the early stages of a cultural trauma is not just "why is this happening to me?" but "why is this happening to us?" The collective identification implied with the term "us" can have several levels of meaning. It can refer to a specific group, a real or imagined community such as a racial or ethnic group, an entire nation, or even a civilization. In the case of Katrina, it was posed most pointedly in reference to regional politics and to African Americans. Explanations as to why the response to the disaster from the federal government proceeded at the pace that it did were often couched in terms of American politics; for example, that a Republican president was reluctant to help a state and a city governed by Democrats. A racial and class dimension was also prominent: some viewed the response to Katrina as evidence that blacks and poor people were not a national priority. There was an even broader interpretation regarding the collective in which it was perceived as the victim, where the "us" was defined as all the people of the affected region. A theological explanation was offered in which the hurricane was understood as an act of divine intervention, the wrath of God imposed on an unworthy humanity. In this explanation, race and class played little role; God's wrath was indiscriminate.

The issue of who is to blame has many levels of meaning and possible designations. Was it an act of God, a force of nature that was the ultimate cause of this disaster?[14] Even if that were the case, was there room to include the human hand? If so, then what role did national and local politics play in the making of the disaster and in the response once it happened? How far into history must one look to answer questions about why the levee system failed? These were all issues that emerged in the public discussion that followed the storm's wrath. Katrina's wake provoked many to look for the hand of God to explain the devastation. This included New Orleans mayor Ray Nagin, who said, "Surely God is mad at America," in explaining the hurricane's destruction in a Martin Luther King Day speech in January 2006.[15] Religious conservatives in the United States and abroad were also quick to see the hand of God in the disaster; radio pastor Pat Robertson claimed it was God's punishment for a liberal stance on abortion, and Steve Lefemine, a South Carolina minister, agreed. Black Muslim minister Louis Farrakhan said the hurricane was God's way of punishing America. Similar references came from around the world. In Israel, one rabbi blamed the hurricane on President Bush's call for withdrawal of Jewish settlers from the Gaza strip, and Al-Qaeda in Iraq said that with the hurricane "God attacked America."

Religious interpretations of disaster have a long history and have been categorized by philosopher Gottfried Leibniz as a form of theodicy, the attempt to reconcile great human suffering with the existence of an all-powerful God.[16] The term was later applied by sociologists Max Weber and Peter Berger to include secular as well as religious accountings of great suffering. Through this prism, some aspects of the public debate over Katrina can be traced back to the "earthquake sermons" of the eighteenth century, in which ministers blamed the sins of their parishioners for natural catastrophes and a broader secular debate was sparked by the Lisbon earthquake of 1755. That earthquake produced a famous exchange between Enlightenment philosophers Voltaire and Rousseau. Responding to a poem Voltaire wrote about the Lisbon earthquake in which he mocked the idea that it occurred as the "result of eternal laws, directing the acts of a free and good God," Rousseau blamed the suffering not on God but on man. He wrote,

[T]he majority of our physical misfortunes are also our work. Without leaving your Lisbon subject, concede, for example, that it was hardly nature that there brought together twenty-thousand houses of six or seven stories. If the residents of this city had been more evenly dispersed and less densely housed, the losses would have been fewer or perhaps none at all.[17]

In this exchange, one can find themes that have come to frame public debates following great human disasters, including Katrina. Writing in the *New York Times Magazine* soon after the 2004 tsunami and just months before Katrina, Susan Neiman recalled the Lisbon earthquake and the debate between Voltaire and Rousseau in a discussion of recent disasters.[18] Five years later, James Wood recalled the same debate when he wrote in the *Times* about a storm that had devastated Haiti.[19] All this reveals how the past helps us make sense of the present.

KATRINA AS CULTURAL TRAUMA

Hurricane Katrina evoked public discussion in the United States. This was not so much because of the force of its winds, or the great destruction the subsequent flooding caused. The public debate following in its wake erupted in response to the less-than-effective relief effort and the role played by local, regional, and federal political authorities in marshaling this effort. An important element in this debate concerned the place of race and social class in conditioning the extent of the suffering and the quality of the response to it. The prime reason for this was that the overwhelming majority of those left behind to suffer the direct force of the storm were poor and black. Although many criticized the lateness of the order to evacuate New Orleans and its surroundings, there were two primary reasons many of those still remaining to face the worst of the hurricane did not flee to safety. The first was history and memory: they had heard and seen all this before and either did not believe what they heard or believed they could wait it out as they had done in the past. (Others did not hear the evacuation order at all because they had no access to radio or television.) The second was that they had no way to leave. Many of those stranded had neither an automobile nor funds to pay for another means of escape. Many waited for buses that never arrived, and still more found themselves trapped in badly equipped shelters such as the Superdome and the Convention Center. It is here that the categories of race and class become important in determining the social distribution of suffering. While the wind and water were relatively indiscriminate in the damage they inflicted, the areas affected by the hurricane were clearly segmented by race and class. According to sociologist Michael Dyson, race was a significant factor in who died and in conditioning how the authorities responded.[20] The legacy of slavery and segregation had left a deep mark on the social geography of the Gulf region and the city of New Orleans. Except for the mansions of the wealthy along the most attractive waterfront areas, the most exposed areas were inhabited by the less well off, by African Americans and poor whites. When the winds came and the levees broke, it was these areas and these residents that were the most affected. The Census Bureau issued statistics of national poverty rates the very day the levees broke in New Orleans, "finding that Orleans Parish had a poverty rate of 23.2 percent, seventh highest among 290 large U.S. counties."[21] African Americans composed 67 percent of the population of New Orleans and 84 percent of those below the poverty line, with most concentrated "in 47 neighborhoods of extreme poverty—that is, neighborhoods where the poverty rate topped 40 percent."[22] This made New Orleans second in the nation on a scale of poverty concentration. During Hurricane Katrina, 38 of these 47 neighborhoods were flooded. Broadening our scope beyond New Orleans to the Gulf states most affected by the storm, "more than 90,000 people in each of the areas stormed by Katrina in Louisiana, Mississippi, and Alabama made less than $10,000 a year. Black folk in these areas were strapped by incomes that were 40 percent less than those earned by whites."[23] Louisiana and Mississippi are the two poorest states in the nation.

When using the concept of cultural trauma, one must ask, "Whose trauma?" Katrina was not only a devastating hurricane that caused extreme amounts of suffering but also a catalyst to a national debate in which foundational values were brought into discussion, and in that sense, it was a cultural trauma. How long-lasting and deep-seated this cultural trauma has been remains something to ponder. The most powerful impact of the hurricane, however, was most clearly felt by African Americans, for a foundational racial cleavage was once again made public on a scale that recalled the heyday of the civil rights movement. The quality of the response by governmental authorities was discussed in the mass media, through the arts and popular culture, and in the halls of government. The U.S. Congress held hearings, survivors organized a "general assembly," and news outlets were filled with Katrina reportage and editorial commentary. Katrina dominated public discussion for weeks after the hurricane. Then came the documentaries, songs, poems, art works and theater pieces, and finally academic articles and books. All of these combined to transform Katrina from a devastating hurricane into an event of great symbolic significance heavily laden with meaning and emotion. Katrina has come to stand for much more than a powerful hurricane; it has come to symbolize governmental failure and, more specifically and controversially, the failure of the white majority to care about the black minority. That the hurricane disproportionately affected poor blacks seems uncontestable, but the notion that race was responsible for the acknowledged failures of the relief efforts is not; this remains a hotly contested issue. In this ongoing discussion, the meaning and place of race in American society has been brought up for debate once again. Were race and racism responsible for the quality of the relief efforts? Was America a racist society? Were government officials racist? What kind of society could allow so many of its citizens to suffer in such a public way for so long? Along with negative attributions like "national trauma" and "national shame," these are expressions of cultural trauma.

TRAUMA FOR WHOM?

While everyone who lost a home, a job, or property had their lives significantly fractured in a way that could be called traumatic, African Americans suffered disproportionately, most especially those at the lower ends of the income and education scales. This helped turn the trauma of the victims into a collective and potential cultural trauma. The images of American citizens so sorely in need opened the possibility for others, and not only African Americans, to identify and empathize with these victims. The images of the destitute and the desperate stranded on roads and rooftops pleading for help recalled for many a long history of mistreatment and abuse with roots reaching back to slavery. These images made it very clear who the victims were. Thus, the first group one can point to in answering the question "whose trauma" is African Americans. It was this group, once again reassembled, that most clearly identified and aligned themselves with the victims, and that then helped propel the issue of mistreatment to the level of national consciousness. African American representatives in Congress were quick to call for an investigation and to call those named responsible to account. African American celebrities, most visibly those in the realm of popular culture such as filmmaker Spike Lee and rap artists Mos Def and Lil Wayne, offered musical and visual condemnation. However, it was rap artist Kanye West's remarks at a nationally televised fund-raiser for Katrina victims soon after the storm that intensified the stakes. West said that President Bush "doesn't care about black people."[24] High-level political figures and influential commentators felt compelled to react. The president's wife, Laura Bush, insisted that her husband was not a racist. His father, former president George H. W. Bush, told CNN that he found those remarks not only wrong but also "vicious." And Barack Obama, then a U.S. senator, said that what he called the "ineptitude" of the rescue and relief efforts was not due to race: "I do not subscribe to the notion that the painfully slow response of FEMA and the Department of Homeland Security was racially based. The ineptitude was color-blind." In a lawyerlike speech, the future president added, "I see no evidence of active malice, but I see a continuation of passive indifference on the part of our government towards the least of these."[25] These carefully measured words are nevertheless very telling. The response of government officials, the upholders of the covenant, was clearly not appropriate, most especially "towards the least of these," that is, to the poor African Americans. Katrina was clearly much more than another disastrous incident; it had become a major event that called for response, explanation, and position-taking from public officials, intellectuals, and commentators through the mass media and other public forums. This helped expand the scope of interest and interested parties far beyond African Americans. The mass media organizations, involved from the outset as more than just means of transmission, were themselves major actors, becoming a carrier group in the cultural trauma process. In addition to journalists and newscasters, various mass media outlets called upon expert commentators and editorial writers to interpret the significance of what was occurring.

Did Katrina evoke a cultural trauma for all Americans? Did this debate reach deeper into the foundations of American identity than the issue of race? Did Katrina shake the very foundations of collective identity and reshape collective memory, like, for example, the assassination of John F. Kennedy? Or was it more like the assassination of Martin Luther King Jr., which rocked the entire nation but left more of a mark on African Americans?[26] Addressing such questions will be part of the task of this book. Answering them requires hindsight and a theoretical vantage point from which to gauge the depth and long-term effects of this event. The theory of cultural trauma provides such a vantage point. Besides being an analytical tool, the theory provides a framework that permits us to retrospectively gather various occurrences and forms of expression and representation, from science to the arts and popular culture, and bring them together around a common incident—a hurricane named Katrina.

To study the depth and breadth of a cultural trauma, one must reconstruct and analyze the narratives that various parties put forward in making their claims about the meaning of the event. In technical terms, this means identifying key carrier groups and analyzing the narratives they construct in order to tell their specific story about the incident and to shape its meaning as such. In other words, the analysis must consider how various significant individuals and groups constructed a trauma narrative, a meaningful story in which trauma played a central, organizing role, and form judgments about how influential and long-standing that narrative will be. In our case, this means in part that we must examine the way in which various persons and groups claiming to represent African Americans told the Katrina story. This type of analysis allows us to gauge the success of an intervention into the national debate. What story, for example, did the filmmaker Spike Lee present in his two long documentaries? How were these evaluated and received? How did they impact the overall understanding of Katrina? What were the themes and variations in the arguments put forth by others claiming to speak for African Americans and other groups? Who was represented and who was left out, and why? Which arguments and which groups were the most successful, and why? It also means identifying and reconstructing the arguments and positions put forth to counter these claims. What were these counterarguments and who made them? All of these questions will be addressed in the following chapters.

First, however, we have to look at how the storm became a disaster, how the story was first told, and what alternative accounts were discarded along the way. This unfolding will require reconstructing and analyzing various mass media accounts, justifying the selection of sources, and drawing out general themes. This is the task of chapter 2. I have decided to utilize the *New York Times* and the *New Orleans Times-Picayune* as my primary sources for the firsthand reconstructions. Their coverage is complemented by that offered on cable and network television, in particular by CNN and NBC, two very important sources of information not only for those watching from around the nation and the world but also for those in the affected areas during the storm itself. Both NBC and CNN had reporters on the scene almost immediately who gave firsthand accounts that are still remembered and referred to. In addition, I examine the accounts provided in the weekly newsmagazines *Time* and *Newsweek*, which, because they operate on a different news cycle than the daily press and attempt to provide more background information to accompany their reportage, offer another perspective. The Internet, with its instant access and free-flowing commentary, adds yet another dimension that I explore and incorporate as much as possible. The possibility of providing video images, both amateur and professional, on sites like YouTube has opened a whole new range of possibilities for social criticism and for making public the performance of those in positions of authority, such as the instantly circulated rage of New Orleans mayor Ray Nagin and the patronizing comments of President Bush. Furthermore, the rap videos by Mos Def and Lil Wayne mentioned previously are readily available for free on YouTube. They are professionally produced and make for exceptionally powerful social criticism. On-the-scene amateur videos and still photographs showing images of flooded streets and suffering citizens, as well as incidents of criminality, violence, and incompetence on the part of authorities, are also readily available. Blogs and blogging generally have become a source of informal and instant commentary as well as a means to mobilize public opinion and protest. Several studies of the "blogosphere" and Katrina have been carried out and will be consulted as well. Internet blogging provides local actors with the opportunity to express their views and thus to counter the images and commentary presented in the mainstream media. Published collections make these viewpoints more generally available and can be considered interventions into the meaning struggle and the cultural trauma process. These various sources constitute my first level of analysis, the real-time and contemporary reconstructions of the hurricane and its aftermath as presented through mass media.

Chapter 3 provides a second level of analysis: a consideration of the debates about the meaning of Katrina and its reach. In it I gather, categorize, and analyze the aesthetic response—that is, the reactions of artists, writers, musicians, filmmakers, and graphic designers—to the hurricane and its meaning. I cannot hope to provide a definitive picture of all the aesthetic responses, as they are many, but rather will attempt to provide a comprehensive account that permits categorization along general lines. Just as in my analysis of the mass media, I present themes that capture the vast range of individual responses made by artists along the entire spectrum of aesthetic representation. The concept of trauma—individual, collective, and cultural—will be important here once again. One of the most notable quotations in the realm of aesthetics and politics in the postwar and post-Holocaust period is the remark made by Theodor Adorno concerning the moral possibility of writing poetry, or of producing any form of artistic representation, after Auschwitz. The moral issue concerns in part whether it is better to remain silent about the suffering of others for fear of exploitation. The issue of exploitation and depreciation with reference to Katrina was one voiced in association with mass media and their multitude of images of poor and powerless victims. The same might be said about aesthetic representation generally, even by those claiming to speak for the victims, thus positioning themselves differently from the mainstream media, where (ostensibly) an ideology of neutrality and objectivity prevails. Beyond the moral issue of whether it is better to remain silent than to speak, Adorno's statement can be transformed into one that asks how it is possible to aesthetically represent extreme suffering and the traumatic at all. Katrina was clearly traumatic for those most directly affected; the issue of how to represent their suffering is an important one—for the creator, for those portrayed, and for the viewer. Mos Def addressed this issue in his music video "Katrina Klap," in which he remarks, "Who cares about rock n' roll when babies can't eat food."

This issue of representation will be a central concern of the fourth chapter and will also be addressed in the conclusion. A second issue in chapter 4 addresses cultural rather than individual and collective trauma. What is the aim of artistic representations of a disaster like Katrina, beyond the moral issues just mentioned? What do these artistic expressions themselves represent—are they a form of political art, intended to persuade audiences toward a particular point of view? To that extent, they are interventions into the meaning struggle and the cultural trauma process. Mos Def's "Katrina Klap" ends with him saying, "Don't talk about it—be about it." The relationship between art and politics, like that between art and suffering, has been long debated. I will only take up those aspects that illuminate the examples I have gathered for this study, but I hope my discussion will add something to that debate.

Commercial interests can never be entirely eliminated in any artistic representation, including those associated with traumatic occurrences. Works like those created by artist Terrance Osborne depicting colorful houses floating away in the storm are meant for sale, even if they may also be said to make a statement about the loss of community and a way of life. While one has difficulty disentangling the commercial from almost any form of contemporary aesthetic representation, one can perhaps differentiate between works that are more commercially driven than others. Documentary films, such as the two made by Spike Lee, are meant to be more independent of commercial interests and the need to entertain than those made for the mainstream cinema. They may also be more outspoken in their political and moral beliefs, however, which makes for another form of selectivity in deciding what is made visible and given voice. The same can be said about entertainment and its value in contemporary popular culture. The music videos of Mos Def and Lil Wayne, no matter how powerful and politically motivated they may be, must be made with entertainment in mind in order to ensure an audience. Academic discussions, books, and articles are likewise not free from the issues of intent and audience, nor are they free from the question of the author's position in regard to what is being portrayed, argued, and defended.

The concluding chapter returns full circle to the theoretical issues raised in this introduction, asking what we have learned from this research. One issue is how and in what way these reflections on Katrina affect the theory of cultural trauma that provides the analytic frame of analysis. Theories are only starting points, and the research process that they help organize always alters the very frameworks that make them possible. Just how the theory of cultural trauma has been modified will form a central part of the concluding chapter.

2

PRINT MEDIA

"To put the national Hurricane Katrina experience in perspective, fewer than several hundred thousand people witnessed the storm in person. For the other 99.8 percent of Americans, the disaster was a media experience with lasting implications for the public opinion and action."

ARIC MAYER IN *OLD AND NEW MEDIA*,
EDITED BY DIANE NEGRA

Hurricane Katrina came to most of the world through the mass media. Even those living in the affected region learned about what was to happen to them through mass-mediated accounts, first through graphic projections broadcast on television and then through local civilian-band radio and the Internet as the storm struck. In this chapter, I will trace the way the hurricane was represented in portions of the mass media and turn Mayer's statement into a question: did Katrina have "lasting implications for the public opinion and action"? The key term here is "lasting," for the short-term implications are beyond doubt.

What began as a traditional storm and potential disaster story with coverage of dire warnings, preparations, and evacuations quickly turned into one of tragedy, desperation, and death. Stories of survival became the major theme.[1] As the hurricane made landfall on the Gulf coast and it appeared that New Orleans, the largest and best-known city in the region, had been spared, media interest focused on the smaller towns and cities along the coast. Then the levees protecting New Orleans failed, and a windstorm unexpectedly became a flood of catastrophic proportions. As the levees burst, so did the established media script; interpretive frameworks shifted as the hours passed and the human drama increased. Katrina became a story of human suffering and of desperate efforts at rescue. With regard to those in authority, it became a story of responsibility and blame. The new situation tested the limits of traditional print reporting and of network broadcasting, opening an opportunity for newer forms of information dispersal to flourish, and for older ones to reconfigure. Issues of race and poverty, not often problematized by mainstream media, were soon thrust into the spotlight. The desperate faces of survivors being broadcast around the globe were mostly black and poor, a fact that became impossible to ignore in the racialized culture of the United States. Connections between race and the quality of organized rescue attempts became a central theme in media representations and discussions. Why did it take so long for help to come? Why were survivors forced to beg for help, holding pleading signs aloft from rooftops and highway overpasses, all of which were represented in compelling photographs and film footage? As this new narrative unfolded, the performance of political authorities and law enforcement personnel became the subject of extensive media coverage. Who was responsible for the obvious inadequacies in providing care and safety for those left in the hurricane's wake? The debate over local and regional authorities, especially in New Orleans and the state of Louisiana, soon spread to the federal hierarchy as well, extending all the way to the presidency.

News reporting was not incidental to the ways in which these authorities understood Katrina and reacted to it. But during the first days of the storm, there was great confusion as to what exactly was happening and how serious the situation was. When levee breaks were first observed by firefighters on the scene in New Orleans and by reporters from the *Times-Picayune*, this information was treated as one among many conflicting reports about the extent of the damage and the threat to the city. There were national news media reporting that New Orleans had "dodged the bullet" and escaped the brunt of the storm. When a FEMA supervisor on the scene attempted to convince his superiors in other parts of the country of the need for an immediate federal response, he was greeted with reluctance because, as one of those officials said, "cable TV had been reporting all afternoon that the city had been spared the big hit."[2]

The mass media, particularly the national news media, were thus a central actor in defining the situation, in determining how serious it was and what could and should be done, and one of the central carrier groups of the evolving trauma drama. This was infuriating to local media outlets. Media personalities themselves became part of the story, as local reporters were treated as heroes for their determination to remain in the city and carry on their professional duties, one of which was contesting claims made by other media sources.[3] In the chaos of the storm and its immediate aftermath, local authorities, including journalists on the scene, had to not only understand what was happening but also convince others up the bureaucratic chain of command of what was occurring and how serious the situation had become. New Orleans mayor Ray Nagin, working out of a command center in a downtown hotel, received a flow of incidental and anecdotal information about the situation in the various parts of the city. From these often conflicting and harrowing reports, his staff had to piece together a coherent picture and convey it to others above and below him in the chain of command. With the main lines of communication out of order, Nagin relied on media reports, as did FEMA director Michael Brown, on the scene in Baton Rouge. Brown would later feel the antipathy, and the power, of the media when he became a symbol of the failures of the rescue effort. Interviewed on CNN, Brown was asked by a reporter, "Do you look at the pictures that are coming out of New Orleans? . . . And do you say, 'I'm proud of the job that FEMA is doing on the ground there in a tough situation'?" To which Brown replied, "I look at these pictures and my heart breaks . . . My heart breaks just like the rest of the country's heart breaks."[4]

Brown learned from TV reportage that thousands of people had spontaneously gathered at the New Orleans Convention Center, something he apparently then forgot to inform his superiors about. In a telling exchange broadcast live over National Public Radio, a reporter confronted Michael Chertoff, the secretary of the newly constituted Department of Homeland Security and the man with ultimate authority over rescue efforts. "We are hearing from our reporter—and he's on another line right now—thousands of people at the convention center in New Orleans with no food, zero . . ." Chertoff replied that food was on the way and added that one should not listen to rumors. The reporter replied, "But, Mr. Secretary, when you say that there is—we shouldn't listen to rumors, these are things coming from reporters who have not only covered many, many other hurricanes; they've covered wars and refugee camps. These aren't rumors. They're seeing thousands of people there."[5] Media accounts were used both to counter what responsible authorities believed and acted upon and to afford that same authority with information and access to the general public. Media representations were thus an important part of the message; a message that was interpreted and used to different ends.

Katrina made front-page news for the *New York Times* on August 29, 2005. A small headline on the top left-hand side announced a powerful storm approaching the Gulf coast and accompanying photographs showed long lines of cars heading out of New Orleans and tourists leaving their French Quarter hotels for the safety of the Superdome. Mention was also made of casinos closing along the Mississippi coast. The story and a map depicting the projected path of the storm detailed the storm's growth. Hurricane Katrina was about to make landfall, and the *Times* reported that Mayor Nagin had ordered a mandatory evacuation for the city and that President Bush, vacationing on his Texas ranch, had just declared a state of emergency for the Gulf coast. The president was said to be actively engaged in following the storm's progress, while urging people in the area to head for higher ground. The *Times* quoted tourists and restaurant and hotel personnel in the city's famous French Quarter. This was the New Orleans the world knew and loved.

The *Times-Picayune* told a different story. The New Orleans paper had been tracking the storm for days, reporting evacuation recommendations and advice from various authorities. The paper's bold headline in its August 28 edition, the last issue before the storm hit, warned, "Katrina Takes Aim." The *Times-Picayune* did not publish another print edition until September 2, when a much reduced and limited edition was printed on presses in another part of the state. A dramatic photograph exists of a water-soaked street-corner newspaper box uncovered from the rubble weeks later. Newspaper staff and their families spent two nights in the paper's downtown building, about one mile from the Superdome, riding out the storm before they were forced to evacuate as the floodwaters rose and about 80 percent of New Orleans found itself underwater. The lights went out in the city on August 29 at 5:10 a.m. Monday morning and the paper's emergency generators were not powerful enough to run the printing presses, although they could support Internet operations.[6] The staff members decamped to several locations and managed to put out a web-based edition each afternoon. Their predicament and professionalism was the subject of a *New York Times* article on September 5.[7] The *Times-Picayune* stayed on the job throughout the storm; many on the staff decided to remain in the city and to put a paper out, even if only online and with no clear conception of who would be reading it.[8] In an interview, Mark Schleifstein, a *Times-Picayune* reporter, offered another account of the relations between various departments and staff members. According to him,

There were about 250 people in the paper's building during the storm and through Monday, including family members, from newborn to elderly in wheelchairs. Monday evening, water began rising around the building and by Tuesday morning, was about 4 feet deep. Decision was made to evacuate in the paper's box trucks. Some of the trucks attempted to go directly to Baton Rouge. Others went across the river to our West Bank bureau, where everybody got out and discussed what to do. Several staffers/ editors decided they would return with at least one of the trucks and set up shop in dry area in the Uptown part of the city, while the rest of our group would head to the *Houma Courier*, which had agreed to set up a temporary newsroom for us that night. That's where I went. That night, the Houma evacuees put out the paper online, basically creating it in pdf format with the *Courier*'s assistance. It was then an afternoon paper and two days later [the *Courier*] agreed to print copies of our paper for several days. Wednesday morning, reporting staffers in Houma moved up to Baton Rouge to the LSU campus, joining the rest of the staff. The group that stayed in New Orleans would drive in and out of the city, and be supplemented by the Baton Rouge contingent, over the next few days. Communication was difficult between all these three locations because of failure of the cell towers and other infrastructure problems.[9]

Besides a commitment to their profession and their paper, one motivation for staying behind while their families and friends evacuated was to learn what was happening to their own homes and property, a motivation shared by many others in the city and surrounding regions. As it was, more than 40 percent of the *Times-Picayune*'s staff lost their homes to the flood.[10] One of the paper's major scoops, the discovery that the levee had broken in the Lakeview district, a relatively affluent and predominantly white neighborhood, occurred because reporters who lived there had checked on their homes. This was the source of one front-page story.[11]

Times-Picayune journalists saw it as their responsibility to get the local story and tell it to their readers, though by this time most of the city's residents had evacuated.[12] They did this in part to tell their audience what it most wanted to know: the extent of the damage in their neighborhoods and what they could expect when they returned. They were also motivated to counter the reports of national news organizations like the *New York Times* and the *Washington Post*, and most specifically CNN and the major television networks. These large "corporate media" were viewed as having "parachuted into the Superdome" to look for the most dramatic scenes, turning the Ninth Ward into the nation's iconic Katrina image. The *Times-*

Picayune at first intended to offset this image with balanced reportage of the city's different neighborhoods and areas, which is to say with coverage across the class and racial lines in this segregated city. But one can detect a subtle shift in the *Times-Picayune*'s focus over time. Rather than centering on the poor and the black from the beginning, which is what they accused the corporate media of doing, the *Times-Picayune* staff eventually ended up with a similar focus primarily because it wanted to record the local story. By the middle of the first week, this meant reporting on those who remained in the city: the poor, the black, and the elderly, as well as the professionals who remained to care for them. The latter contingent included both those who carried out their duties heroically under impossible conditions, as was true of many hospital workers, and those who failed miserably to do so, like the members of the police force who joined in the lawlessness they were sworn to prevent. Looting, said *Times-Picayune* editor Jim Amoss, was news, dramatic and real, and while it might not have occurred in every corner of the city, it was felt to be a prevalent danger.

Of course, the media itself contributed to this feeling with the words and images it disseminated daily. This was especially the case with television, to be discussed in a separate chapter. Threatening images of desperate people and groups of young black men moving through the desolate New Orleans streets filled the evening TV news programs, accompanied by phrases like "a state of anarchy" or "a night of hell." Media outlets seemed to compete with one another in representing what they described as the collapse of social order, conveyed by reports of sniper fire and interviews with harried and distraught police and other city officials. At one point, as we will see, the networks cautioned each other about the possible effects of their focus on the drama of violence. The print media was a bit more subdued.

The words "Hurricane Edition" and two distress flags were at the top of the *Times-Picayune* web edition posted in the afternoon of August 29. Its bold headline proclaimed, "Ground Zero." The main concern seemed to be providing information about the impending storm and advising residents, especially those still in the city, on where to go. A parish-by-parish list of shelters appeared along with stories of the massive evacuation in progress, including one about three nursing-home residents who had died while being evacuated on a bus bound for Baton Rouge. The mayor's "first ever" mandatory evacuation order issued at 9:30 that morning was another featured story. The dramatic "Ground Zero" headline on the front page was clear reference to the 2001 attack on New York's World Trade Center, a way of putting the two cities and the two disasters on the same plane. Beneath this headline was a large photograph of the Superdome with the caption, "At least 10,000 find refuge at the Superdome," and the explanation, "These are people without enough money or luck to leave town."[13] To the observant, the photographs revealed exactly who remained in the city. An ominous bold text on page A3 warned that "a surge would likely top New Orleans Levee System" and thus that major flooding was a distinct possibility. An unsigned editorial predicted, "[T]he worst stories from Hurricane Katrina aren't likely to involve how long people had to sit stalled in traffic. They'll probably come from those who stayed behind." These words proved prophetic.

Within this information, one can identify a subtle shift in narrative focus from evacuees and storm devastation to rescue efforts and the fate of those left behind. The commitment to local coverage brought with it the demand for on-the-scene reportage centered on the lives and interests of those close at hand. This was a focus the paper shared with on-the-scene cable and network television coverage, but there were important differences between them, as will be discussed in detail in a later chapter. For now, one can say that the local reporters had more knowledge of and commitment to the city and its people. In addition, all members of the *Times-Picayune* staff suffered from the storm; many lost their homes and automobiles, yet at the same time they shared a professional interest in the drama. Soon after the winds died down, those remaining reporters and photographers were out collecting material, bearing witness to the suffering and devastation. One adventurous photographer moving through the city as the waters were rising came upon a family trapped on their front porch and surrounded by rushing water. As they yelled for help, the *Times-Picayune* photographer faced a dilemma common for "cool media" like television and film in hot situations: "If I can't help them, is it okay to shoot their picture?"[14] In this case, the photographer took the picture and then went for help.[15] Another pair of reporters who stayed behind in New Orleans happened upon groups of individuals, including police and firefighters, looting a local superstore; instead of taking pictures, the reporters joined in to gather some much-needed supplies. Minutes later they had second thoughts and decided to return the things they took, after which they shot a photograph of a New Orleans police officer with an armload of DVDs coming out of the store.[16] The photograph soon appeared in the *Times-Picayune* and caused a great public outcry. This photograph and many others helped give rise to another major theme in local and national news coverage: the breakdown of law and order. This theme would bring accusations of media bias when it appeared that many of the broadcast images pictured young black males as the main perpetrators.

The August 30 web edition of the *Times-Picayune* had the word "Cata-strophic" in huge black letters across its front page. Just above it in bold red lettering were the words "Katrina: The Storm We've Always Feared," with the same two distress flags alongside the paper's masthead and the notation "Hurricane Edition." The lead stories and accompanying photographs were of a middle-class white family in Lakeview who "lost everything, cars, art, furniture"; rescue efforts in Chalmette, where an elderly white woman was shown being taken from her attic; and two black men awaiting transport from the Ninth Ward. An attempt at racial and class balance appears to be present in this reportage, though the interviews confirmed that much was also determined by circumstance in a very chaotic situation. There followed a two-page photo report.

The August 31 front page was dominated by the bold-faced headline "Under Water," with reports about levee failure and continued flooding. The theme of law and order was introduced through a headline on page A2, "Weariness, danger, death take hold in drowned city." The accompanying text contained a quotation from the city's director of homeland security, who claimed, "There are gangs of armed men in the city moving around the city." This alarming statement was followed a few pages later by the bold headline "Looters leave nothing behind in storm's wake," and then by the even more disheartening statement, "Police officers seen joining in." This was accompanied by the photograph of the uniformed NOPD police officer (black) carrying DVDs from a local store. Underneath this story was an additional article headlined "Looter shoots NO officer in the head." The juxtaposition must have been intentional. These stories were capped by an unsigned editorial that began, "In the hellish aftermath of hurricane Katrina, it is imperative to restore some semblance of order to our wounded hometown . . . Unfathomably, some New Orleans police officers and fire fighters, as well as harbor police joined a crazed mob in looting the Wal-Mart on Tchoupitoulas Street." The editorial closed with an observation and a plea: "This community has months of back-breaking work ahead to clean up and rebuild. Residents must be able to trust that they can return to their mangled homes in safety, and they must be able to trust the officers who were sworn to protect them." Here we can see a clear reference to the covenant, that specifically American relation between authority and citizenry. The police are holders of office, sworn to uphold the principles of justice and equality before the law. They are bound by duty and are the recipients of trust from those they are chosen to represent. This relationship was severely tested in Katrina's aftermath.

No mention was made of the reporters and their initial impulse to join in the looting, or of the dilemma they faced, namely, how to acquire essential supplies when all the stores were closed. This would later become part of a national discussion about behavior during emergency situations and the depiction of violators in the mass media.

A front-page story in the August 30 web edition of the *Times-Picayune* announced that the surging water had flooded neighborhoods in the city's Ninth Ward and St. Bernard Parish farther down the levee, and that a breach in the Lakeview levee threatened to inundate the inner city itself. The paper's previous predictions about the levees had proved correct. In terms of the city's racial makeup, mention of the Ninth Ward and St. Bernard Parish is significant in that one is predominantly black and the other white. The rising water was in this sense indiscriminate, and this was the way the story was framed, a point made stronger in the juxtaposition of photographs of white residents being rescued and photos of blacks heading for the shelters. A headline on page A6 noted, "Hundreds believed to be trapped in their attics." For those with knowledge of past hurricanes in the region, this brought frightening images to mind. The paper's inner pages contained photographs and stories from the primarily white suburb Slidell, which was reported as being under five feet of water, and a two-page photo spread of the Ninth Ward, which had also flooded. The issue of looting and the problem of lawlessness were relegated at this point to the back pages. A headline on page A10 announced, "Widespread looting hits abandoned businesses—Lack of police after storm leaves stores vulnerable." This was accompanied by large photographs of people, all of them black and most of them young males, carrying various forms of merchandise along the street.

Two contested themes would later emerge from this: the prevalence of looting by black males and the inability of local police to maintain order. The *Times-Picayune* had previously reported that "young men exited the Coleman clothing store . . . struggling under the weight of fully laden cardboard boxes and plastic bags . . . four young women slipped out of the Magnolia Discount convenience store . . . and loaded pilfered boxes into a waiting car." This was printed under the headline, "Scenes from a broken city."[17]

VICTIMS AND VILLAINS

Villains, heroes, victims, and perpetrators: these are the central characters in mediated dramatic representation. This is true for all levels, from the local paper to the national and the corporate, and for textual as well as visual representation. What shifts are not the categories or cast of characters but the emphasis and focus. Personalization and stereotyping were two of the centrifugal forces at play in media characterizations of Katrina. The *New York Times* continued to frame its Katrina story in terms of storm and rough weather. The front page of its August 30 edition was dominated by a photograph of rescue workers transporting people in a boat on a flooded street in the Ninth Ward, while a headline declared, "Hurricane Katrina slams into Gulf Coast; Dozens are dead" (www.nytimes.com/2005/08/30 /national/30storm.html). While the accompanying story showed the breadth of the suffering, including the statement that "some of the worst damage reports came from east of New Orleans," the main photos in the print edition concentrated on the Ninth Ward (the Internet edition included an interactive feature that contained an array of photos from the entire area). That bad weather was still the focus was confirmed by an article about "storm cycles" and an editorial headlined "Nature's revenge." However, there were seeds of a shift in focus as the editors wrote, "The damage caused by a hurricane like Katrina is almost always called a natural disaster. But it is also unnatural, in the sense that much of it is self-inflicted. New Orleans is no exception . . . its politicians and planners must rethink the bad policies that contributed to the city's vulnerability." Like many other cities, New Orleans, as one commentator put it, was built in defiance of nature,[18] a thought which recalls the discussion between Rousseau and Voltaire described in the previous chapter. Built in a hurricane corridor on land that in many places is below sea level and exposed to water on three sides, New Orleans is a natural disaster waiting to happen. Given this risk, the editors suggest, measures should have been taken to lessen the impending calamity, and that was where the responsibility of those in authority lay. Bad policies and bad decisions had let down those in this vulnerable position, and the most vulnerable of the vulnerable suffered the most.

The *New York Times* of August 31 gave Hurricane Katrina full front-page coverage, including the main headline, "New Orleans Is Inundated as 2 Levees Fail; Much of Gulf Coast Crippled; Toll Rises." The extent of the devastation was now gaining a central place in its coverage, as authorities searched for words and images to make this understandable to outsiders. "It looks like Hiroshima is what it looks like," Governor Haley Barbour of Mississippi told the *Times.* The notion of war-inflicted damage and war zone photography would soon become a dominant form of representation, verbal and visual. In the coming days, newspapers and television coverage would depict helpless people as victims and as "refugees." The *New York Times* and others further pursued war zone references, with helicopters, armored vehicles, and military personnel, along with burning buildings and smoke-filled skies. This can be explained in part by the fact that some of those taking the pictures were experienced combat photographers and also by the fact that part of New Orleans and the Mississippi coast indeed looked like a war zone. But clearly, as war zone journalists knew, there is more drama in helicopters, smoke, and bleeding victims than in the more routine relief efforts. It was the dramatic photograph and film sequence that made the "news." Photographic images showing physical devastation and human suffering dominated the news and the newspapers. Another photograph on the *Times* front page this day showed a weeping woman and the body of her dead husband behind her. Besides suffering victims, another photographic subject was the heroic efforts of rescue workers, with an inside headline that announced Katrina had necessitated the "largest relief effort since 9/11."[19] Rescue was also the subject of the day's editorial lead comment. Under the headline "New Orleans in Peril," the editors wrote, "Right now it looks as if rescuing New Orleans will be a task much more daunting than any city has faced since the San Francisco fire of 1906. It must be a mission for us all."[20]

The enormity of the catastrophe, the relief effort, and the politics behind it all were headlined in the *New York Times* of September 1: "Bush Sees Long Recovery for New Orleans; 30,000 Troops in Largest Relief Effort. Higher Toll Seen." This was accompanied by a large photograph of desperate people evacuating the city by walking along abandoned railroad tracks, in another reference to refugees fleeing a war zone. In this telling photograph, those fleeing were all black and the two rescue workers pictured were both white. The lead story on the front page also highlighted looting and looters. The story opened with a paragraph-long sentence, "Chaos gripped New Orleans on Wednesday as looters ran wild, food and water supplies dwindled, bodies floated in the flood waters, the evacuation of the Superdome began and officials said there was no choice but to abandon the city devastated by Hurricane Katrina, perhaps for months." Inside the paper were stories and images of that chaos and the response by authorities. One headline, "A City of Troubles," was accompanied by a photograph showing state troopers in full combat gear, and another headline noted, "Owners take up arms as looters press their advantage." This story included a photograph of two armed shop owners, a statement by Mayor Nagin that "The looters are starting to get closer to heavily populated areas," and a report that Louisiana Governor Blanco was "furious" about the looting. In another reference to New York and 9/11, a New Orleans city council member said, "Had New York been closed off on 9/11, who can say what they would have done," in effect asking the *Times* readers what they would have done in a city that was closed and abandoned. The *Times* turned this apparent "chaos" into an issue of political leadership by adding an image of President Bush peering out the window of Air Force One and an editorial headlined "Waiting for a leader." The editorial comment began, "George W. Bush gave one of the worst speeches of his life yesterday . . . he advised the public that anybody who wanted to help should send cash, grinned and promised that everything would work out in the end." It closed by saying, "It would be some comfort to think that, as Mr. Bush cheerily announced, America 'will be a stronger place' for enduring the crisis. Complacency will no longer suffice, especially if experts are right in warning that global warming may increase the intensity of future hurricanes. But since this administration won't acknowledge that global warming exists, the chances of leadership seem minimal."

Hurricane Katrina was here moved to another level and given meaning with reference to another political debate. For the *New York Times*, Katrina was clearly more than a hurricane; it was becoming a symbol or symptom of something much deeper, with many levels of meaning and interpretation contained in that depth.

RELIEF AND RESCUE

The Thursday, September 1, web edition of the *Times-Picayune* was concerned with depth of another kind. Its headline read, "Hitting Bottom," with the accompanying story offering a hopeful observation that the floodwaters had finally reached their apogee. Yet the large photograph under this headline showed something else. It was of a man carrying his possessions toward the Superdome, which by this point had become a symbol of refuge and despair. Seeking refuge in the beleaguered Superdome was indeed hitting bottom. By this time close to twenty thousand people were taking shelter in the giant sports stadium, and although this was the third time it had been used as a hurricane shelter, its provisions were scarce, as there had been no substantial preparations such as gathering large stockpiles of food, water, or generator fuel. In addition, two relatively large holes in the roof caused by the high winds had allowed water to leak down on those taking shelter. Beneath the *Times-Picayune* headline and alongside the photo were two feature stories, one running down each side of the first page. On one side was reportage that engineers were punching holes in the levees to speed drainage, and on the other side a story of survival headlined "Nightmare in the 9th Ward all too real for one woman." This story was a harrowing survivor's tale of a woman haunted by images of "dead babies and women and young and old men with tattered T-shirts or graying temples" floating along the streets of her neighborhood. Survivors in the Superdome and in neighborhoods like the Lower Ninth Ward now came to dominate firsthand reportage.

The day's editorial asked the leading question, "Where is the cavalry?" in reference to a great American myth, presented in many Western films, where beleaguered settlers surrounded by marauding "Indians" hope to hear the rallying sound of the bugle and see the cavalry charge to their rescue. In New Orleans, these marauders were the looters, the vigilantes chasing them, and the armed, deranged, and angry citizens taking random shots at rescue workers. Unfortunately, this broader picture of the marauders was narrowed down in the minds of the public to the young black males pictured in the media. It was they who in the public mind threatened the city. The editorial called for the National Guard to be the cavalry: "New Orleans needs a show of force. Now. Until the city is inundated with law enforcement officers, from every level of government, the anarchy of the past few days will only worsen." This view was reinforced by the final sentence of the editorial: "Virtually everyone involved in public safety has failed the people left in New Orleans who are trying desperately to survive." Jim Amoss, the paper's editor, did not write this editorial, but he stood by it.[21] He added, however, that while this sense of a city out of control was pervasive at the time, there were of course neighborhoods where relative quiet prevailed.

The call for help was repeated in bold headlines in the *Times-Picayune* the next day, September 2, when the words "Help Us, Please" covered the front page. This headline was followed by the subheadline "After the disaster, chaos and lawlessness rule the streets." A dramatic photograph of a black woman on her knees crying out for help was accompanied by the caption "A distraught Angela Perkins screams 'Help us, please!' outside the Ernest N. Morial Convention Center . . ." The rest of the newspaper was filled with reportage of violence and looting and a photograph of armed police and dogs standing over three young black men lying face-down on the ground: "Police K-9 officers hold a group of looting suspects at gunpoint after arresting them." The boldface text on page 11 proclaimed, "Crackdown on Chaos—New Orleans police fought to take the city back," captioning a photograph of police searching for looters. A full page of photographs lay under the headline "Desperation and Destruction," with the main photograph showing a young black woman and a group of young children at the Convention Center. This was becoming a common motif: desperate black women and children depicted as victims in need of aid, and looting young black men as villains in need of discipline and punishment.

Times-Picayune reporters remaining in town and on the job added analysis to the more descriptive stories of suffering and survival. On September 2 the issue of who was responsible for the devastation was raised, a theme that would dominate the discussion in the coming weeks. One article, carrying the headline "Levees' weakness well-known before breaches," began by stating, "lack of political will, funds cited in failure." It contained a map of the city showing the various levee breaches and consequent flooding, and provided evidence that Katrina was more than a natural disaster, as much of the damage could be traced to bad decisions and the failures of various authorities, a point made also by the *New York Times*. Now that Katrina was identified as a social disaster, the issue of who was responsible was firmly on the agenda, and the Army Corps of Engineers, the agency responsible for building and maintaining the levee system that protected the city and its environs from floods, was to become the main culprit. Hurricane Katrina would soon become known locally as the "Federal Flood," with the Corps of Engineers, along with local and national political leaders, counting as the responsible federal agents.

The rest of the paper was filled with a now common theme: looting and violence, or "Despair in the Streets" as the headline on page 12 declared over a set of photographs of desperate individuals, most of them black, outside the Convention Center. Along with the Superdome, the Convention Center had become the gathering place for those remaining in the city, a fact overlooked by responsible authorities for some time. The one elderly white man in the photograph stands out among the many blacks. The theme of "who was responsible?" was continued in the September 3 edition, which carried the main headline "First Water, Now Fire" across the first page, a reference both biblical and secular as sporadic fires had broken out across the city. Another headline announced, "Bush stunned by condition of New Orleans," with a small photograph of the president comforting a distraught woman during his visit to the Mississippi Gulf coast. The article carried a hint of criticism of political engagement in the relief efforts. This theme was continued on page 5, where a headline proclaimed, "Even Republicans decrying president's response to crisis." While political response and responsibility was prominently discussed on one side of page 1, the other main story concerned violence and relief. The headline read "More guns, buses, relief roll into the city," with the guns referring to National Guard troops, not illicit weapons. In an edition filled with hurricane stories, the appearance of three pages covering sports news must have provided a sense of relief and the promise that the situation would return to normal in this sports-centered city. The other noteworthy addition was the appearance of a full-page advertisement by State Farm Insurance agency, announcing that "we're here to help." This was the only form of advertising to appear in the hurricane editions.

The promise of respite and relief was emphasized the following day, Sunday, September 4, as the bold headline proclaimed, "Help At Last." The story began, "After five days, thousands of anguished storm victims finally have a reason to hope." This optimism was tempered, however, by the accompanying photograph with the caption, "helicopters evacuate people in need of medical help as crowds of others displaced by Hurricane Katrina pile into buses . . ." The dominant image was still that of a war zone, a lone helicopter hovering close to the ground in an atmosphere of smoke and devastation, with lines of tired and distressed individuals awaiting evacuation. Signs of hope and inspiration could also be found in the accompanying stories lining the first page. One headline read, "Authorities regaining grip on the city," while a story about the power of song in times of need carried the headline, "Amid chaos, a rare voice of strength."[22] Accompanied by a photograph of a black woman singing on the street with her arms raised to the heavens, the article told of a woman breaking spontaneously into a gospel song as a means of countering despair and desperation. The lyrics included this line: "When the storm of life is raging, Stand by me, Stand by me." The woman was identified by name and said to be from the Ninth Ward. The story continued pages later under the headline, "Bystander says song prevented possible rioting." The theme of responsibility for the disaster was continued on page 2, which carried the headline, "As calm settles over N.O., outrage grows in Washington," with the text highlighting congressional criticism of the performance of FEMA and President Bush. The rest of the paper, with the exception of two pages of sports, focused on survivors and victims and addressed an emerging concern: the numbers of the dead.

The headline on Monday, September 5, proclaimed the area's "7th Day of Hell," with the subheading "A week of horror ends with more evacuations and uncertainty." The story on page 2 continued along these lines: "Body count in state provides initial death toll," with fifty-nine dead bodies so far in the state morgue. In contrast, a story under the headline "Parade returns to French Quarter" included a series of photographs that depicted the happy faces of people dancing in the street. Those celebrating were all white and young. The theme of recovery would soon come to dominate the newspaper's pages, and the race and class of the actors represented would shift dramatically from black and poor to white and middle class. The remaining pages of the September 5 edition, however, returned to the more familiar stories of survival. The final section depicted the previous week's front pages, with their bold headlines of disaster and despair.

Recovery and return was headlined the following day, September 6, as the front-page headline boldly announced, "Coming Home," accompanied by a large photograph of two women, both white, in their Jefferson Parish home. The issue of September 7 headlined the more familiar disaster story, with "Disease, Fire Threaten City" proclaimed in bold type across the front page. The text highlighted the danger provided by the toxic waters still flooding most of the city, and the message was clear: all those remaining should leave. This was countered, however, by an interview with Ray Nagin bearing the headline, "Mayor Nagin stays optimistic and defiant," although he too was "begging" those still in the city to leave. This message was re-inforced the following day in a story headlined "Clear Out or Else," and on September 9 a story headlined "After Hell, high water holdouts pried loose," accompanied by a photograph of people being forced out of their homes by soldiers, stated, "Few souls remain in shell of a city."

While covering some of the same ground, the New York Times was raising more general issues. With its main first-page headline of September 2, "Despair and lawlessness grip New Orleans as thousands remain stranded in squalor," the Times highlighted disorder and desperation. A smaller head-line read, "Bodies and Fear in the Streets." These words, presenting the by now familiar picture of a city in disarray, were set alongside a large photograph of a body floating under an overpass while a woman offers water to a dog above. The symbolism is compelling: water as the source of life and death, depending on where one stood. There was more obvious symbolism as well; both the body in the floodwater and the stranded woman on the overpass above were black. This and the other predominant images suggested that the "despair and lawlessness" gripping New Orleans had deep racial roots. Beneath this photograph was another photo showing a row of distraught individuals facing an armed soldier charged with keeping them orderly. The caption read, "Victims of Hurricane Katrina trying to get onto buses for Houston . . ." The accompanying text identified something that was already obvious: "The victims . . . were largely black and poor, those who toiled in the background of the tourist havens, living in tumbledown neigh-borhoods." The article was based on viewpoints expressed in Washington by members of the Congressional Black Caucus, but what was said should have been obvious to anyone viewing the images coming out of New Orleans, either the still photographs in the daily press or those continuously shown on television. One could ask: who were the villains and who were the victims? Who were the vandals, the looters, the causes of disorder? Who were the victims and what, after all, were they victims of? Were they victims of the hurricane, the quality of the relief efforts, the criminality on the streets? All this was left ambiguous.

The themes of responsibility and victimhood would dominate news coverage over the next weeks and months. While the *Times-Picayune* remained largely true to its concern with local issues and the plight of individual survivors and those who did not survive, the *New York Times* raised the stakes and the level of abstraction. The suffering individuals were identified as a group, a "race" in American terms, while those responsible for the catastrophe resided in the nation's capital. A *Times* article carried the headline, "From margins of society to center of the tragedy." From this perspective, it took a major catastrophe and tragedy to bring the issue of race and poverty into the national spotlight. The hurricane made the plight of those on the margins visible for all who cared to see, something that, though tragic, provided the nation with an opportunity, a chance to make amends. The connection between race and poverty (though not the opportunity) was commented on in a *Times* interview with sociologist Christopher Jencks the following Sunday. Jencks "found himself surprised" at the images he saw coming out of New Orleans, saying, "This is a pretty graphic illustration of who gets left behind in this society—in a literal way." In attempting to understand his own surprise, Jencks continued, "Maybe it's just an in-the-face version of something I already knew . . . All the people who don't get out, or don't have the resources, or don't believe the warning are African American. It's not that it is at odds with the way I see American society . . . But it's at odds with the way I want to see American society."[23]

The interview was part of an article written by Jason DeParle, a reporter specializing in issues surrounding poverty and author of the book *American Dream*. It was accompanied by a graphic that illustrated the opening sentence: "The white people got out. Most of them anyway. One lived on high ground and fled to higher. One was low and made lower." The graph revealed that 28 percent of the people of New Orleans live in poverty, and of those, 84 percent are black. A final illustration showed how this impacted car ownership and the possibility of evacuating a city in danger where the prime evacuation plan was based on people driving their own vehicles to safety. The most obvious of the hurricane's victims, those who remained behind and suffered not only the loss of home and livelihood, as did many hundreds of thousands, white and black, wealthy and poor, were here designated as those poor blacks who faced the humiliation and despair of being stigmatized and badly treated in a society where their existence was already marginal and bare. What then were the causes of this suffering? Was it the hurricane itself, the ensuing flood, or those in charge of relief and rescue? If it was the latter, then how far up the chain of command did this responsibility go?

FROM NATURAL TO SOCIAL DISASTER

That there was blame to be placed for the quality of the relief effort became apparent soon after the narrative shifted from a storm story and a natural disaster to a social drama of survival and rescue. This occurred most notably as the levees failed and the floodwaters inundated New Orleans. The potential failure of the levee system was something the *Times-Picayune* had reported long before it happened, though President Bush would famously remark afterward that "no one predicted" that the levees would fail.[24] The paper had repeated this during its hurricane coverage,[25] and the story was then picked up by the *New York Times* and other national media. The levee break meant that the Army Corps of Engineers would bear much of the responsibility for the ensuing flood. McQuaid and Schleifstein would conclude their book *Path of Destruction* by describing the results of an independent evaluation of the Corps of Engineers' responsibility for the disaster. To those carrying out the study,

> New Orleans was not just the victim of a few bad calculations. It was a latter-day version of the *Titanic*'s sinking or NASA's two space shuttle disasters, where a cascade of bad decisions had tragically doomed ambitious technology. They concluded that the Corps, abetted by its junior partners, the local agencies, had failed as an institution long before the levees actually collapsed.[26]

The levees failed because of design problems, for which the Army Corps of Engineers were ultimately responsible. In this sense, Katrina *was* a federal flood.

The *New York Times* focused much of its attention on Washington and the presidency when it came to deciding where ultimate responsibility rested. From the perspective of national politics, Katrina was the first real test of the president's second term. Already on September 1 the *Times* editors were looking for leadership and found it wanting in the White House; by September 3 they had widened the list of responsible parties to include Congress as well. Beneath the headline of its lead editorial, "Katrina's assault on Washington," the author wrote, "Do not be misled by Congress's approval of $10.5 billion in relief for the Hurricane Katrina victims. That's prompted by the graphic shock of the news coverage from New Orleans and the region, where the devastation catapults daily, in heartbreaking contrast with the slo-mo bumbling of government." The news media, in other words, had done its job in exposing the human side of the storm, forcing a recalcitrant federal government into action. In the closing paragraph, the editors made clear that those with an ideological preference for small government and cutting taxes bore responsibility for the disaster. For the *Times*, Katrina was a clear sign that something was wrong with these ideas. "Congress and the president had better get the message, an extraordinary time is upon the nation. The annihilation of New Orleans is an irrefutable sign that the national tax-cut party is over. So is the idea that American voters cannot be required to accept sacrifice or inconvenience no matter how great the crisis. The country is better than that."

Given the subsequent rise of the Tea Party, this argument seems optimistic at best today. However that may be, the *Times* reported a general feeling of dissatisfaction with the governmental response to the hurricane, something that the Tea Party would later turn into a general mistrust of government. Under the headline "Storm and Crisis," which had by now become a regular heading, and the equally telling subhead "Eyes on America," the paper reported, "Across the U.S. and abroad, outrage, shame and disbelief at response."[27] The point was that Katrina was a test and a showcase and that America had failed, and failed badly. While nature may have provided the initial force, politics and ideology bore major responsibility for the disaster. Here the *Times* was putting forward the liberal position that government and the public sector were responsible for collective well-being and that these responsibilities could only be carried out with sufficient funding. The *Times* received some unexpected support for this viewpoint the following week when conservative commentator George Will wrote in *Newsweek*, "Katrina provided a teaching moment. This is a liberal hour in that it illustrates the indispensability, and dignity, of the public sector." However, Will went on to modify this point by also saying, "It is also a conservative hour, dramatizing the prudence of pessimism, and the fact that the first business of government, on which *everything* depends, is security."[28] Katrina was thus much more than a hurricane or a natural disaster; it was a political test, of ideas and ideology.

In her September 3 column, "United States of Shame," regular *Times* commentator Maureen Dowd wrote, "America is once more plunged into a snake pit of anarchy, death, looting, raping, marauding thugs, suffering innocents, a shattered infrastructure, a gutted police force, insufficient troop levels and criminally negligent government planning." The response to Hurricane Katrina had shown the country at its worst, she wrote, and the whole world was watching. Like the *Times* editors, Dowd placed the blame on politics: "Stuff happens. And when you combine limited government with incompetent government, lethal stuff happens."[29] The use of such terms as "shame," "catastrophe," and "failure" are just the type of negative attributes that Neil Smelser identifies as essential indicators of cultural trauma.[30] Such terms filled the mass media accounts of Hurricane Katrina and its aftermath. *Newsweek*, for example, called Katrina a "National Shame" on its front cover of September 19, 2005, a cover dominated by the face of a young black child rescued from her flooded New Orleans home.

The long-term impact on the individuals, the region, and the nation were themes that emerged in the *New York Times'* still very extensive Katrina coverage in the following days. Though Katrina was pushed off the main headline by the death of Supreme Court chief justice William Rehnquist, the centerpiece of the front page on Sunday, September 4, was a large photograph of soldiers and police entering the Convention Center, with the caption "Bush pledges more troops . . ." Accompanying text confirmed that seven thousand more soldiers were on their way to New Orleans at the same time that two hundred New Orleans police had walked off the job. The responsibility for law and order was shifting from local to federal authority. The remainder of the paper was filled with accounts of the extent of the damage and the problem of coping with its effects. One article, "Storm will have a long-term emotional effect on some, experts say," contained quotations from psychologists and sociologists, including Kai Erikson, Lee Clarke, and Steve Kroll-Smith, about the projected effects of the hurricane. The accompanying photograph showed an armed soldier standing by as a young girl carried food from a relief station. The photograph could have been from some war-torn country in Africa rather than a U.S. city. Disaster expert Clarke remarked that the impact of Hurricane Katrina was new and different from anything America had previously gone through and that past experiences might not be sufficient for understanding its impact. "I don't know that we've seen anything like this . . . It is outside experience in some ways . . ."[31] The idea of something that happens being "outside experience" can be a symptom of trauma, one Clarke locates at the collective level. Erikson brought that concept to the individual level when he told the *Times* reporter: "People don't know until something like this comes along how much the shape of their house, the texture of their house, the mood of their neighborhood, are important parts of who they are . . . you have no idea how much they mean to you until they are gone or permanently altered."

A TRAUMATIC OCCURRENCE

The statements by Clarke and Erikson bring us back to the discussion in the first chapter, namely, the idea of collective trauma and the relation between individual and collective trauma. Something being "outside experience" recalls the classical notion of trauma as understood by Freud and his later followers like Cathy Caruth.[32] In this formulation, trauma is beyond experience, an intrusion into the mind's sensibilities that cannot be easily absorbed. While this notion of trauma restricts itself to individual experience, a disaster like Katrina can raise the experience of trauma to embrace a collectivity, perhaps even a nation. Katrina may at one level be like other hurricanes and floods, a disaster that can be categorized and compared with others. But it is also unlike others, its emotional impact pushing or breaking the boundaries of the category to which it belongs. In this sense, Katrina is more than a disaster in the established meaning of the term. In my terms, it is a traumatic occurrence, an incident so shocking that it shakes taken-for-granted assumptions of experience and opens the grounds of collective life to individual and collective reflection. This will not happen spontaneously or automatically, however. The shock must be articulated, represented, made coherent, and communicated in compelling ways. It must be interpreted, shaped, and made meaningful. This appears to be what is occurring in these media accounts, which grasp for narrative form to make sense out of catastrophe, again marking the media as an important carrier group in the social construction of disaster and the cultural trauma process.

This framing helps explain phrases like "Is this America?" and the references to other places on the globe—to the "Third World," to much poorer countries, to Somalia and Haiti, to the devastation brought by war—to something unfamiliar to most U.S. citizens. It also explains the controversial application of the term "refugees" to those fleeing New Orleans in a second wave as floodwaters, not the hurricane, engulfed the city. Such a term, some would later argue, should not be applied in America, to American citizens. As we will discuss, many saw racism hidden in the usage of the term.[33] This debate points to the release of deeply held beliefs and emotions in response to an incident so damaging that it shook the very foundations of collective identity. There is no question that Katrina caused individual trauma, and as Erikson suggests in the quotation above and throughout his writing, collective trauma for those in its direct path. The issue is whether or not Katrina, understood not merely as a hurricane and flood but as a traumatic incident, resulted in a cultural trauma, a long-term and far-reaching public debate where the foundations of collective identity are touched upon. Many reporters and media commentators attempted to make this transformation from traumatic incident to cultural trauma occur, and for a time, in the heat of the media cycle, a debate about collective identity did indeed take place. We will be asking about the impact of such attempts, how successful they were, and how long-standing.

There is another sociological point to be highlighted before returning to the narrative: namely, the role of intellectuals and professionals in helping shape the meaning of an incident, in helping make an incident into an event and, possibly, a cultural trauma.[34] In constructing an event out of an array of occurrences, journalists, editors, publishers, and the others who make up what we call the mass media rely on various experts in interpreting and confirming what is indeed happening. Such experts, usually professionals of one sort or another, act as agents in constructing a general account; they also give the weight of their authority to the story as it is being constructed and communicated. A reporter is a wordsmith, hammering out a coherent framework from past scripts to make sense of what is seemingly chaotic and random. In the process, journalists often call upon experts to bolster their stories, to lend authority, and to add levels of meaning. In several of the previous examples, the experts called upon added depth and authority to the story line about the hurricane's long-term effects. The main idea behind the headline and the story line was that Katrina was much more than a storm in the ordinary meaning of the term. It had (or so it was claimed) fractured the boundaries of a category of experience, something which these experts reinforced with their commentary. Expert testimony and the scripted story lines that guide news reporting are important factors in turning an incident into a significant event. How significant, and what sort of event this will be, is contingent upon the way these accounts are structured. The frames of reference and the rhetorical devices used are important in determining how compelling the accounts will be for particular audiences. In one example, expert testimony on long-term social and psychological impact lends support to the general aim of bearing witness, creating empathy, and garnering sympathy for the victims of this storm from readers who are at a safe social and geographic distance.

The newsweeklies *Time* and *Newsweek* also contributed to turning a disastrous storm into something much more. Neither of the magazines covered Katrina in their September 5 issues; their content was determined more by production scheduling than current events. The cover photograph of *Newsweek*'s September 12 edition showed a young black woman with two young children in her arms, with a caption reading, "A Katrina refugee and her two children New Orleans, Sept. 1, 2005." Above the photograph were the phrases "Pray for Us," "Horror in New Orleans," and "The Relief Fiasco," all of which summarized quite well what could be found inside. Coverage began with a "photo essay" featuring "images of devastation, anguish and survival"; this was followed by "Crisis and Chaos: New Orleans' descent into despair," "The White House: The price Bush will pay," and "Health Crisis: The dangers are just beginning." With the exception of the last story, these were all themes familiar from the daily news coverage. The longer signed essays also followed themes and used phrases from the daily press. Regular columnist Jonathan Alter offered advice on how to save New Orleans, which reiterated the view that tax cuts would only worsen the problems currently facing the city, but then made the wider claim that "New Orleans will need the love of the nation it does so much to enliven. To save this city—or any city where people are hurting—requires rejecting . . . heedless tax cuts and I-got-mine selfishness in favor of a sense of community and competence that all Americans deserve."[35]

"IS THIS AMERICA?"

An "Opinion" essay by Georgia congressman John Lewis searched for a reference point to grasp what had happened. "I went to Somalia in 1992 and I saw little babies dying before my eyes. This reminded me of Somalia. But this is America. We are not a Third World country. This is an embarrassment. It's a shame. It's a national disgrace."[36] The phrase "This is America?" would be one often repeated in later debates about Katrina's meaning. The question graced several exhibitions of post-Katrina artwork, such as one at the Louisiana State Museum on Jackson Square in central New Orleans that will be discussed in chapter 3. What is the intention behind this question; why is this reminder necessary? Was it because natural disasters of this scope are unusual in this country but are more common in other parts of the world? Or was it because this was a social disaster of the sort that is not supposed to happen here? Lewis' intention appears to be the latter, that such things should not happen in the United States, that "we" can and should do better.

The designations "embarrassment," "shame," and "national disgrace" are powerful negative attributions intended to raise the stakes in public debate and to promote action. They appeal to a sense of collective responsibility and guilt, implying that what happened to New Orleans happened in America to Americans; that as Americans, we have a responsibility to react. This *is* America, after all. While the photographs of the poor and the black may call to mind other parts of the globe, as they did for John Lewis, the underlying idea behind them and the accompanying text was to remind readers that these are your fellow citizens, Americans like yourselves. The images shock after all *because* this is America. On the other hand, such images, as well as the context in which they are viewed—over evening coffee in a comfortable middle-class home, perhaps—might well promote distance between the viewer and the object, especially when they can be easily categorized as different, as poor and black, for example, and thus not like me. The move from "me" to "we," from self to collective interest, to provoke an empathetic response in its readers appears as the driving motive behind *Newsweek*'s Katrina coverage.

Newsweek succeeded in creating this identification and sense of empathy, if the letters to the editor in response to the September 12 issue are any indication. The magazine reported that it received more than one thousand letters, "many of them heated. Most took the Bush administration to task for what they said was the inept response to the catastrophe."[37] One Connecticut woman wrote,

> Choosing a cover photo that captures the essence of your lead story each week can't be easy. However, the photo of the woman with her two children on your Sept. 12 cover grabbed both my attention and my heart. In her arms, along with her children, she is holding the same baby blanket that my older son has. Seeing the identical blanket made me realize that it could easily have been my family with our home gone and our lives uprooted, with just a security blanket left to hold.[38]

The selection of a young woman with her children seems an appropriate choice from the point of view of creating empathy. Motherhood has universal appeal and young children are generally perceived as innocent and worthy of protection. The fact that the young mother was black created some potential barriers in a country where racial classification is so predominant, a factor which must have influenced the choice of a young mother with children. The face of a young African American man would have opened another range of possible interpretations, which might not have achieved the desired effect. As a symbol, clothing is important, but who could have known that a baby blanket would carry so much meaning?

REPAIR AND REDEMPTION

The September 19 issue of *Newsweek* had another empathetic image on its cover, a large close-up of "one-year-old Faith Figueroa, rescued from her flooded home in the Lower Ninth Ward, New Orleans." Faith, a black child with large watery eyes staring straight into the camera, a tear streaming down her cheek, was the picture of innocence in need. Over this image were positioned the phrases "Why Bush Failed" and "Children of the Storm"; to the side was written, "Poverty, Race & Katrina" and "Lessons of a National Shame." The critical nature of these stories was introduced and explained by the journal's editor, Mark Whitaker,[39] who put forth his views on the role of the media in times of crisis:

> It's an old reflex of the American press, strengthened by 9/11. After the horror of a national tragedy, we look for uplifting stories of redemption. And so it was last week in New Orleans . . . But while the awful images of the deadly storm and its wretched aftermath are still fresh in all our minds, we believe it's also the role of the media to keep asking hard questions, to at least begin a search for answers. The first question is how such a catastrophe could have been allowed to happen. Even more troubling, the second question is why in the richest country in the world, there was still a population in harm's way so poor and helpless that many had no resources to escape or cope with the storm when it hit.[40]

The central themes of the September 19 issue were the failures of the relief effort, the suffering of those left behind, and the shortcomings of the Bush administration in providing aid. The main story, however, was contained in Jonathan Alter's essay, "The Other America," which was accompanied by a large photograph of an elderly black woman in obvious need who sat draped in an American flag. The photo was captioned "Left Behind." The title, as well as the photograph, recalls the civil rights era and Michael Harrington's 1962 book with the same title, one of the key texts that spurred student revolts and the Great Society programs of the Johnson administration. The article begins by pointing out that poverty in America is not new, but rather "an enduring shame," which Katrina has once again exposed to full public view. "It takes a hurricane," Alter wrote. "It takes a catastrophe like Katrina to strip away the old evasions, hypocrisies and not-so-benign neglect."[41] Though horrible, the devastation offers an opportunity, a chance to face the reality of poverty and make it right: "This disaster may offer a chance to start a skirmish, or at least make Washington think harder about why part of the richest country on earth looks like the Third World." With an unacknowledged nod to Harrington, Alter remarked that much has changed for the better in the United States over the past four decades, with Medicaid and Social Security "all but eliminat[ing] poverty among the elderly" and food stamps and changes in tax laws helping the very poor.[42] However, despite these improvements, things have gotten worse since the 1990s. Alter documented poverty rates in the United States that stood at 12.7 percent of the population, "the highest in the developed world and more than twice as high as in most other industrialized countries."[43] After suggesting their fellow Americans knew little about the poor, Alter described them, revealing that in sheer number there are more whites than blacks who fall below the poverty line, yet nearly 25 percent of all African Americans in the United States can be categorized as poor, compared to 8 percent of whites and 22 percent of Hispanics.[44] The graphics accompanying the text illustrate the numbers of the poor in America by age, race, marital status, and national origin. Finally, the issue of poverty in America is localized to New Orleans, where relevant figures are shown for each neighborhood. Alter stated at the outset, "The question now is whether the floodwaters create a sea change in public perceptions," that is, an opportunity to once again tackle "the enduring shame" of poverty in America.[45] He concluded by saying that Washington still wanted to cut aid to the poor and offer tax cuts to the wealthy, policies that would only make the situation of America's poor worse. "What kind of president does George W. Bush want to be? . . . Katrina gives Bush an only-Nixon-could-go-to-China opportunity, if he wants it."[46] The fate of poverty in America lies in Washington. Alter's intent was clear: to influence Newsweek's readers and through them to sway public opinion with the thought that Katrina offered the country an opportunity to face and begin to make right a long-enduring problem. Catastrophe and trauma had opened old wounds, but also new possibilities.

The more politically conservative Time magazine took a decidedly different approach in its Katrina coverage, though its photographic images covered much the same ground. The cover of its first Katrina issue was draped in black, made more dramatic by the magazine title in dark red and the text "An American Tragedy" in stark red and white.[47] The photograph showed two black women trapped in the flood, calling for help. The table of contents announced a fifty-two-page special report, while an accompanying photograph pictured three elderly blacks under the word "Forgotten" with the caption, "Evacuees, still waiting for help five days after Katrina hit."[48] The list of the contents followed much the same pattern and evoked similar themes as *Newsweek*: the photographic "Portfolio" portrayed "Images of frustration and grief." There followed a series of articles: "The Aftermath: A city is failed in its time of need," "How It Happened," "Rebuilding," and "How you can help," which offered a list of charities where readers could send money. A lead essay by regular columnist Joe Klein, titled "Listen to what Katrina is saying," preceded the photo gallery. It pointed once again to the idea that there was something to be learned from the catastrophe. For Klein, the message Katrina imparted was not that different from the one offered by Alter and *Newsweek*: "having celebrated our individuality to a fault for half a century, we now should pay greater attention to the common weal,"[49] though without real specification of how this should happen. The placement of this message was perhaps meant to prepare the reader for the shocking photographs to follow. The first photograph in the portfolio showed a young black mother and child standing in the rain with their belongings, with the bold caption "An American Tragedy." What exactly was the tragedy? If this woman and child were the victims, then who were the responsible agents? This was followed by an aerial photograph of flooded New Orleans, then a close-up photograph of a young white man in tears, with the explanation that he was exhausted after having rescued people in Waveland, Mississippi. An aerial photograph from the Mississippi coast was next, showing the devastating damage done by the winds and water surge. It was an image from a war zone, like the aftermath of carpet bombing, or a surrealistic painting of apocalypse; there was nothing left of a row of houses but a smoldering fire and a car floating in a swimming pool. The next two photographs were clearly meant to complement one another: the first showed suspected looters being arrested by New Orleans police officers, most of whom were also black; the other was titled "Helping Hands" and showed a group of people, white and black, helping a Mississippi convenience-store owner clean up his shop. The final photographs returned to New Orleans, with a picture of a crowd of jostling people, young and black, attempting to board buses from the Superdome that was captioned "An Angry Exodus." The gallery begins and ends with women in need; these are clearly the victims, but who was to blame for their fate?

An answer is suggested in the article by Amanda Ripley: "Hurricanes kill people because we refuse to settle out of their way."[50] This is essentially the same argument made about the Lisbon earthquake by Rousseau in his counter to Voltaire, mentioned in the opening chapter. It is the rationalist argument and also one of common sense: if one is not in harm's way, then one will not get harmed. Those in need of rescue were those who put themselves in harm's way. Either they did not leave when ordered to do so, or they should not have been there in the first place: "It's a fool's paradise, hurricane expert says of New Orleans."[51] Who bears ultimate responsibility for the settlement and the population of New Orleans? Is it those individuals who live there, choosing the city even in the knowledge that it lies in the path of powerful storms? Does responsibility lie with the authorities and officials who designed the buildings, the levee system, and the emergency evacuation plans? Does responsibility go higher up the authoritative chain? Does it lie with the Congress and the president? "Would it have mattered," Ripley asked, "if the Corps [of Army Engineers] had gotten all the money it had asked for" to fix the levee system aimed at protecting New Orleans?[52] The answer, she maintained, was uncertain. The real issue, according to Ripley, was America's general level of preparedness with regard to impending disaster, "the big one" to come. "Katrina was a big, vicious storm . . . But Katrina was not the worst-case scenario. Katrina was a test."[53] The rhetorical question put forward by Klein, "what does Katrina tell us?," is here answered with another question, "is America prepared?" One could assume from the essay that Katrina told us America was not prepared, and that, while one can blame the victims for living in a "fool's paradise," it was still the responsibility of those in positions of leadership and authority to provide some protection from their folly. This was the lesson, or at least one lesson, to be learned from Katrina.

The issue of who and what was responsible for the disaster was also the subject of the next section of *Time*'s Katrina coverage, "An American Tragedy." Under the heading "The Fragile Gulf," the section opened with the words "The Gulf Coast . . . is one of the most delicate ecosystems on earth— and one of the most economically important areas in the United States. Can these two realities co-exist?" A two-page graphic illustrating the ecosystem and its vulnerability followed, bearing the title "A Calamity Waiting to Happen." The aim was to portray the Gulf coast as "America's soft underbelly," where the situation worsens with each passing year, as "the shriveled Louisiana coastline is dying a slow death at human hands."[54] That is, the economic value of the region was fast undermining its ecological sustainability. Given a fundamental tension between the need to develop and to sustain a fragile ecosystem, the people of the region could not be held entirely responsible for being there; they were necessary to at least one side of the equation. This being the case, blame must lie elsewhere, with management and leadership, that is, with those responsible for maintaining the delicate balance and for sustainable development. The situation, it would seem, called for vision as well as strong leadership, though *Time* did not draw any conclusions from its presentation. The economic costs of Katrina were the subject of the next section, "The Billion Dollar Blow Out," which discussed the economic impact of the storm on the region and the nation. A section on how to manage the emergency then followed.

Under the heading "Here's What to Do," four community leaders and emergency management experts who had experienced similar disasters were asked for their opinions. One of them was the former mayor of an Indonesian city devastated by a tsunami. He began with the candid statement, "I have to admit that I was one of the first people to break into grocery stores the day after the tsunami. I did it because help had not arrived and people were hungry."[55] He then stressed how important it was that basic needs be provided for as soon as possible after a catastrophe. An emergency management official from Florida with experience from Hurricane Andrew put the matter of aid in temporal terms: "The first 72 hours after a disaster is the 'golden' period. That is when victims should start receiving food, water, ice and medication. If you are not visible within 72 hours, you will have chaos . . . Every minute counts." A third expert disagreed, at least regarding what the first priority of emergency managers ought to be. She stated, "You are there to protect people's lives and property . . . The first thing you have to do is stabilize the situation and get help to people."

The cover of the September 19 issue of *Time* featured another stark image of a black female covering her mouth with her hands in horror and the words "System Failure" streaked across the photo in bright yellow-green. The cover also promised "An investigation into what went wrong in New Orleans." The caption inside explained the cover photograph: "Earline Scott reacts to a fire . . ." The issue's table of contents relating to Katrina was again labeled "An American Tragedy." It promised the following: "Portfolio: Images of Katrina's Devastation," "Who is to Blame: A Time Probe finds confusion and incompetence at all levels," and "Bush—Anatomy of an insular White House." The "probe" listed four places where the "system broke down": the mayor's office in New Orleans, the Louisiana governor's office, FEMA and its director Michael Brown, and the Department of Homeland Security, the organization with direct responsibility for the rescue efforts.[56] The article on the president found Bush "living too much in the bubble," claiming, "A bungled initial response exposed the perils of a rigid, insular White House."[57] The next section, titled "Looking Ahead," discussed the

White House strategy to repair the president's image. The final Katrina section was called "Mopping New Orleans" and focused on the cleanup. This was the last Katrina discussion, as the September 26 issue turned to Iraq.[58]

CONCLUSION

The print media were important in telling the Katrina story, turning a devastating flood into an event of national significance. Local and national news media gave coherence and direction to a chaotic flow of incidents; they provided a narrative framework that permitted readers to make sense out of a wild array of occurrences. This narrative framework did not emerge out of nowhere; it built upon tried and tested scripts that were adjusted and expanded as the story was being told. In the process, a variety of themes emerged that helped shape the public's understanding of these occurrences. Journalists and commentators scrambled to find words and phrases to fit what they saw and heard. As this all took place in the heat of the moment, their interpretations were often infused with emotion, stemming from the frightening power of the occurrences themselves. Finding the right phrases and images to help others make sense of what was occurring before their eyes was a struggle that tested the boundaries of established scripts. On the scene, reporters were not describing something they could easily distance themselves from; they were trying to make sense out of horrifying scenes of destruction, death, and despair, as well as heroic and not-so-heroic human responses. Often this included their own responses. How these stories and images would eventually be interpreted by their audience is of course a very complicated matter and something we will be discussing throughout this book. Audiences are multilayered and varied, and though journalists do have some idea about who follows their work, this idea remains an abstraction, "the general reader." The general reader of the *New York Times*, however, is presumably different from that conceptualized by a reporter for the *Times-Picayune*. The newsweeklies appear to have a more concise picture of their audience, at least as far as one can glean from their pitch and tone and from the advertising they carry. In all cases, however, an attempt is made to frame the stories and present the images in a particular way, to influence what is seen and read through projecting what Stuart Hall has called a "preferred reading."[59]

Katrina coverage began as a traditional rough-weather story, something for The Weather Channel, concerned with naming and tracking a potential storm threat to a region of the country. Here, visual media—television and print graphics—were predominant. Television was especially effective with its sophisticated color graphics and sound, as will be discussed in detail in a following chapter. As the threat became greater, the attention and audience grew in proportion, engaging not merely the curious and those directly threatened, but the interest of the nation, up to and including the president, whose views were commented upon even before the storm made its most powerful landfall. Textual material gained significance in pace; there was a potential story to be backgrounded and elaborated upon. National attention was called to the Gulf coast and especially to the city of New Orleans, as the mass media in all its forms and formats rushed in with the approaching wind. A Category 5 hurricane heading for a vulnerable American city was "news" of national significance. The devastating impact of the storm and the subsequent flooding of New Orleans after its protective levee system failed changed the interpretive framework, from a weather story to human drama. The focus of media attention shifted as well, from damage and destruction to the struggle for survival, to victims and who they were and to what and who was responsible for their misery. In the process, the self-defined role of the media changed, at least for some, from providing information and description to witnessing and advocacy.

How do we explain these shifts? Were they primarily a function of the massive destruction, the number of those affected? Or was it something else: the significance of the city, its people—qualities rather than quantities? Did a hurricane called Katrina become a symbol with many layers of embedded meaning simply because of the numbers of deaths, of those displaced, of houses and livelihoods affected? I think not. While numbers matter and by all measures Hurricane Katrina caused massive damage and killed more than a thousand people, by themselves the numbers do not fully explain the attention given. Something more than the numbers was at stake, the most obvious being the city of New Orleans and its place in the American imagination. But there is more to it than that. As the floodwaters rose, it became increasingly clear that basic social categories—age, race, class, and gender—were significant factors in determining who remained in the city, who survived, who would return, and under what conditions. In addition, some fundamental aspects of the modern American experience were exposed to public view, as the winds and floodwaters stripped bare some of the surface layers of daily life. These included a tension, built into what some see as the most sacred of American documents, the Constitution of the United States, between the rights of the federal government and those of the states to provide care and protection to the citizenry. The general confusion as to who was in charge was in part a result of this uncertainty, which was not a minor factor in the bungled relief efforts. It seemed clear to many that the covenant sanctifying the relation between the American government and its people, if not shattered, had been severely damaged. Related to this was another foundational distinction, that between public and private interests and organizations. What role could and should a private organization such as the Red Cross play in relief efforts? What role might family networks or volunteers play? Who could make that sort of decision, and by what right? The exposure of these foundational values and distinctions are related to the process of cultural trauma, and we will discuss this connection and its workings in Katina in the concluding chapter of the book.

ARTS AND POPULAR CULTURE

"Names are talismans of memory too—Katrina, Camille.
Perhaps this is why we name our storms."

NATASHA TRETHEWEY

New Orleans promotes itself and is represented by others—journalists, writers, artists, musicians—as exotic, as different. Drawing upon this image was central to calling attention to the storm as a meaningful danger to a national audience. After all, there were plenty of other dangers to be concerned about, from terrorist threats to the war in Iraq. Had Katrina missed New Orleans and wrecked only the Mississippi coast, it would have been treated differently by the mass media. New Orleans widened the potential audience, as it increased the number of those at risk. But a threatened city is not enough to explain all the attention, for one could reasonably ask why not Detroit, another decimated American city? One answer has to do with image: the projected image of New Orleans is cultural and intangible; that it is an irreplaceable national treasure. Detroit is associated with products, automobiles, material things that can be produced elsewhere. That is a process seen as natural to capitalism: products come and go, as do those who make them. There is also the difference between a sudden shock—a storm or flood—and the slow, long-term decline of an industrial city like Detroit, where there are now more than twenty thousand homeless living on the streets.[1] In contrast, a sudden natural disaster, which turned into a social disaster due to broken levees and inadequate relief efforts, brought national attention. One could pose the question differently, as did Jim Amoss of the *Times-Picayune*, in an interview with me: why didn't New Orleans get greater attention? Amoss conjectured that it was because it is a southern city, on the periphery and marginal to the centers of power in Washington, New York, or even Los Angeles. Had a Katrina-like natural disaster hit one of those cities, coverage would have been even greater. Yet there is something about New Orleans that attracts attention, and part of that something is that it acts as a cultural magnet, drawing people with an interest in aesthetic representation and expression to its vulnerable urban landscape.

In this chapter, I analyze representations of Katrina in the arts and popular culture, almost all of them focused on the city of New Orleans. There are several aims in this presentation; the first is to be as comprehensive as possible while at the same time providing a framework to make the vast amount of material comprehensible. Since I am interested in Katrina as a traumatic occurrence with the potential to alter the established boundaries of experience, I will address the question of whether or not it was so powerful as to "exert narrative pressure on even the most stable of genres," as Diane Negra asks, concerning what she calls "cataclysmic national events."[2] Or as Aric Mayer put it, was post-Katrina New Orleans a site that "seemed to defy and elude the available means of media representation"?[3] Did any difficulty in representation produce an unfinished agenda, opening the possibility for dissenting voices to enter the mainstream of aesthetic representation? Was Katrina so powerful that it burst the borders and boundaries of established modes of representation in the arts and popular culture? Or, put differently, how did established genres shape interpretation of Katrina, in what ways, and to what ends? Are certain film and television forms subject to change and contestation when representing the disaster, or have standard codes and conventions proved resilient enough to evade modification in the face of the ideological and cultural exposure Hurricane Katrina has come to represent?

A word on definition: I purposely combine what are sometimes thought of as separate fields of aesthetic representation, the arts and popular culture, in order to avoid addressing what has been a long-debated distinction. I have entered into this debate elsewhere,[4] but see no reason to do so in this context. Rather, I am interested here in the aesthetic response to Katrina by those engaged in traditional artistic practices, like painting, literature, and theater, and in less traditional ones, such as the graphic arts, photography, popular music, film, and video. Included with a discussion of individual works and performances will be an analysis of modes of presentation, such as organized exhibitions and mass-mediated performances, to address the issue of how the mode of presentation might influence the meaning or interpretation of what is presented or performed. I begin with an ongoing exhibition in the center of New Orleans that is meant to represent Hurricane Katrina to the many people who visit the city.

The issue of how to represent complex phenomena in a relatively simple format, bounded by space and the attention of viewers, is a problem faced by all those who compile exhibitions, give lectures, or broadcast the news. An exhibition is an arrangement and a selection, with the intention of representing something to an audience that is at once anonymous and anticipated. One does not know who exactly will walk in but makes an educated guess about those who are most likely to do so. These issues were faced by the organizers of *Katrina and Beyond*, a more or less permanent exhibition at the Louisiana State Museum in central New Orleans, which I visited in January 2012, more than six years after the storm. In the style of many contemporary exhibitions, especially those that wish to broaden their appeal, it makes use of a multimedia format featuring actual television broadcasts and sound effects such as howling winds and raging waters to project direct experience, as well as interactive installations and more traditional displays of art and artifacts. The general aim is to reveal New Orleans as a city built in a precarious location, where "living with hurricanes," as the subtitle of the exhibition declares, is part of its condition. The story of Katrina is thus placed in context, in which the constant threat of raging wind and water has shaped the history of the region and the city.

The exhibition is located on the first floor of a fine old building owned by the Louisiana State Museum at one corner of Jackson Square in the French Quarter. This is the heart of the tourist district and thus many of the visitors are likely to be spontaneous drop-ins, though many local residents have come as well. The stated theme is "Resilience," as declared by a poster that greets the visitor upon entry, yet another nearby poster asks the pointed question, "Is this America?" Resilience is represented as the way the people of the region have learned to cope with ecological vulnerability and the idea that Katrina was only one, albeit an extraordinary exemplar, of many tests. Although it is set in the context of other natural and manufactured threats, Hurricane Katrina dominates the exhibition. One enters through a narrowed passageway that contains a dramatic video presentation of the howling wind and rushing water. Cars and houses float by as frightful sights and sounds fill the hall. From here, one enters a large room where video installations covering various aspects of the response are meant to reveal the resilience of those people who remained in the city during the storm. One theme is titled "Heroes" and features taped interviews with men and women (all black) who helped others during the storm and after; another, called "Hospitals," recounts harrowing tales of hardship and dedication by hospital staff (largely white), who persevered under extreme conditions, without fresh food, water, and electricity. These installations are placed together with artifacts chosen to represent some of the devastation, such as a door with a large white X sprayed onto it to indicate a dead body inside, a wall panel with graffiti markings, a diary etched onto a wall that records days stuck inside an attic, clothing muddied by the rising water, a T-shirt inscribed with the words "make levees not guns," the remains of Fats Domino's piano, and chairs from the Superdome. All of these are meant to reflect, represent, and recall the hurricane's effect. In this setting and displayed in this way, they count as folk art: aesthetic expressions not meant as artworks when they were created, but that have become such works through their placement in a museum exhibition. In this category, I would also count as folk art the markings of the hurricane, such as the black stain of the water line, and the markings made by rescue workers that were left on houses even after renovation to recall what had once been. Many of those rebuilding their homes have left such markings intact. Included also would be the thousands of useless refrigerators left by the roadside with messages of protest and despair written on them. The sullied refrigerator became for many a symbol of the countless frustrations faced by those who returned after the storm. As one returning *Times-Picayune* journalist wrote in October 2005, "Refrigerators are poignant symbols of our city's destruction and our government's inertia; many are now painted with political slogans."[5]

There are no perpetrators represented in this exhibition; if there is a perpetrator it is the force of nature, which is represented through the images of wind and water and the interactive installations that show how the failing levees caused flooding of various neighborhoods. This is made social through mention of the double-edged problem of dealing with river flooding, which led to the creation of the levee system, and with the storms and tides of the Gulf of Mexico. Dealing with the one led to problems with the other; dredging canals and building levees took away some natural protection from the wind and water of the Gulf. Balancing the two needs has been a historic issue. As for victims, the people of the region are portrayed as resilient in facing this near impossible natural situation and making the most of a tough geographical location. In this resilience one finds both everyday perseverance and extraordinary heroes like the individuals represented in the video installations, though little is mentioned of villains and opportunists. There is little mention of crime and looting, which was a major theme in media news reporting. The video installations attempt to show the indiscriminate nature of the devastation and the multiracial nature of the response and rescue.

Yet the leading question "Is this America?" points in another direction: not to resilience in the face of the challenges of a hostile environment, but to the responsibilities of government and to the founding ideals of the sacred covenant between a people and its governing authority. What exactly does "America" mean here? How would one know if this was America or not? Does America stand for the moral agreement, the covenant between a government and its citizenry "conceived in justice, written in liberty, bound in union," to use Lyndon Johnson's words quoted in the opening chapter? America is imagined here to be a moral community where an elected government cares for its people. The question is asked against the backdrop of images of enormous devastation and suffering and seems to suggest that this covenant between the government and the people was broken, that in the aftermath of Hurricane Katrina the response by representative authority was not American, but something other, something less. If this is the case, then the exhibition suggests a perpetrator and a victim—the government and the people.

KATRINA AS MUSIC

Among many other things, the Katrina exhibition at the Louisiana State Museum reveals that the wetlands to the south of the city were long recognized as an important natural barrier against the wind and water coming out of the Gulf of Mexico. Protecting and restoring these wetlands was a long-standing political issue, and local New Orleans musicians were already organizing to protest their destruction in the months prior to Katrina. A group of well-known musicians, including Dr. John, Cyril Neville, and Monk Boudreaux, were brought together to produce an album that eventually was called *Voices of the Wetlands*. It was released in the aftermath of Katrina and got lost in the storm. As Neville put it, "By the time people paid attention to it, there were about nine million Katrina records out there." In recounting its history, George Porter, another of the musicians on the record, said that it became "just another hurricane record."[6] In a telling and useful remark, Porter added, "I think that's the reason it wasn't heard by more of the right people. I don't believe this record was really intended for the everyday record-buying public. I think it was meant to be heard by the powers that be. People who can change something." This remark is telling because it gives an important insight into the intentions of the artists, or at least this one, in making the "nine million Katrina records out there." Many of these "Katrina records" are from benefit concerts, where well-known and less-known musicians contributed their words and voices to help the victims of the storm. As such, many of the recordings have no direct connection to the hurricane, but were nevertheless meant to impact its aftermath and in that sense can be said to be "political" performances, even while the music itself might not be especially political in content. In contrast, *Voices of the Wetlands* is not directly related to Hurricane Katrina, having been recorded prior to it, but was political in that it was created for a purpose, to create awareness and to be heard by "people who can change something." These features all point to useful distinctions in categorizing the massive artistic response to Katrina, musical and otherwise. One may thus distinguish between musical text and performance with an intentionally political purpose and that which is not intentionally political but may have a political context; further, one can distinguish those artistic expressions directly addressing the experience of the hurricane and its aftermath and those that do not.

Alongside food, music has been long recognized as a distinguishing characteristic of New Orleans and the surrounding region. The mix of various regional and ethnic traditions has produced a rich and vibrant musical scene that draws musicians and audiences from all parts of the nation and the world. The New Orleans musical scene differs from others in the United States and elsewhere in that it is not primarily driven by commercial interests or an organized "culture industry" like in New York or Los Angeles. A musician doesn't come to the city to "make it big." Much like in some European cities of similar size, New Orleans music is more rooted in neighborhoods and local institutional networks, which support it and attract outsiders. These include clubs, bars, coffee shops, small recording studios and record labels, magazines, and the like. Then there are also the streets themselves. Spurred on by a tourist industry for which music has long been a resource in advertisements and other representations of the city, and by those tourists who respond to their call, the streets of the city, most particularly the French Quarter and the surrounding areas, remain an arena for musical performance. On any given day in New Orleans, one can find dozens of street performers along Royal Street and around Jackson Square in the heart of the French Quarter. They are there to pick up change from tourists, but street performance also serves as a training and testing ground for young musicians, local as well as migrant.

Apart from this setting are the outlying neighborhoods such as Treme, Bywater, and the Lower Ninth Ward, which have their own club cultures and music scenes, and often see themselves as representing the true heart of New Orleans musical expression. Jazz is said to have its origins in the bars and bordellos of Storyville, a mythical district once located near the French Quarter, but Fats Domino's world-famous rocking piano, which mixed the rolling melodies of Dixieland and the blues with the emerging rhythms of rock in the 1950s, came out of the Lower Ninth Ward. The close-lying neighborhoods of New Orleans have also produced rap artists such as Juvenile and Lil Wayne, and one must distinguish between someone who comes from a neighborhood and a music rooted in a neighborhood.[7] Bywater is also in the Ninth Ward (a ward being a political rather than geographical designation) and is home to an alternative music scene that mixes black and white traditions, like those that put together the *Voices of the Wetlands* album described above. The two areas of the ward are separated by the wide Industrial Canal and thus are very separate and distinct; though they are not far from each other geographically, they are distant socially. Residents of the Lower Ninth Ward tend to be very rooted, with families tightly knit over generations, a factor that has been invoked to explain why so many of them remained during Katrina. They had rarely left the area, did not have access to family networks in other parts of the state, and had nowhere else to go. Bywater, on the other hand, is land-linked to central New Orleans, an easy bike ride along the river from the French Quarter and Frenchmen Street, a traditional location of the "alternative" New Orleans music scene. It is one of the main musical alternatives to the French Quarter, Bourbon Street, and mainstream tourism, including the "nostalgia music" presented there. Bywater is thus more accessible to a more transitory younger generation in search of musical roots and cheap housing. Young whites moving into the Lower Ninth would draw raised eyebrows in a way they would not in Bywater, where they encounter less resistance and suspicion. The discussion about the "end of New Orleans music" tends to focus on the Lower Ninth Ward and its club culture. Statistics showing the numbers of persons returning to each New Orleans neighborhood give support to such concerns. A *Times-Picayune* front-page story in April 2008 pointed out that the city had lost more than one hundred thousand voters during the previous year and that the number of African Americans had sharply diminished, especially in neighborhoods like Gentilly and the Lower Ninth. This was later reconfirmed in a survey reported in the *New York Times* in 2010: only 34 percent of the pre-Katrina population had returned to the Lower Ninth, as compared to close to 80 percent in those neighborhoods dominated by whites.[8]

To this, one must add the annual music festivals, such as the Jazz and Voodoo Fests, where local and national musicians play in the atmosphere of a state fair. The Jazz Fest in late April comes shortly after Mardi Gras and lasts over two weekends, bringing with it another throng of tourists to the city, though of a slightly different kind than those who come for Mardi Gras. Though named Jazz Fest after the city's most commonly associated musical genre, the festival includes all kinds of music and musicians, including widely known performers like Bob Dylan and Bruce Springsteen. In contrast, the French Quarter Festival in early April and the Voodoo Fest are largely local affairs and are free of charge. The Voodoo Fest is celebrated at the end of October and beginning of November, combining Halloween, All Saints, and All Souls days. In November 2005 an abbreviated version marked the first post-Katrina musical celebration.[9] The Jazz Fest of 2006 was also abbreviated, though it was much appreciated as a major step in the city's recovery. Though its attendance of three hundred thousand was a good deal lower than it had been before the hurricane the previous year, the fact that it happened at all was seen as a major step forward and a great psychological boost.[10] The presence of Springsteen and other prominent musicians, along with the return of many local musicians, meant that one of the centerpieces of the New Orleans musical experience had not been washed away with the storm.

Along with other commentators, John Swenson proposes that musicians and music were a catalyst in the rebuilding process during the long months following Katrina.[11] Associations like the New Orleans Musicians Hurricane Relief Fund and Tipitina's Foundation, along with more informal networks, helped organize the removal and rebuilding of members' homes, replaced instruments, and rebuilt clubs.[12] There is a Musicians' Village north of Bywater with houses built with the help of funding from musicians' benefits. While this may have helped some individuals (while excluding others), it was the reopening of venues, from the Ogden Museum of Southern Art near Lee Circle in the business district to the bars and clubs in the various outlying neighborhoods, that helped provide a sense of hope that there was a future and a means of accomplishing the monumental tasks that faced them. As unlikely as it may sound, a museum of art played such a role for one particular audience. "The museum became a meeting place to find out where your family and friends were," said the Ogden's Libra LaGrone. "After 9/11, people posted pictures and signs of all their friends. Well after Katrina, people were coming to the museum to hear the music, have a drink and find out where all their friends were."[13]

Place and space, as well as material objects, take on enhanced meaning for those displaced after a catastrophe. Returning home or to a specific part of a city, neighborhood, bar or club, or even a museum can bring an unexpected flow of emotion. In his very personal observations and reflections upon his return to New Orleans in the weeks after the storm, first published as daily columns in the *Times-Picayune*, journalist Chris Rose recounts many instances of this as he moved around the city.[14] A very powerful example is recorded in Spike Lee's Katrina documentary *When the Levees Broke*. Lee was permitted to film the moments when the mother of his musical director, the trumpeter Terence Blanchard, first entered her devastated home after having fled New Orleans' Pontchartrain Park neighborhood. Mrs. Blanchard broke down in her son's arms as she walked through the house, where all of her furniture and personal items were tossed randomly about. With a voice cracking with emotion, she says, "That china closet doesn't have any business being over here; why is it there by the wall?" Everyday life is ordered, and material objects are part of that order. When they are not where they are supposed to be, one gets disoriented. Chris Rose describes such feelings in his chronicles.

Feelings of displacement, of things not being where they should be, can be multiplied exponentially when a whole city is affected. Describing performances of his Katrina-related music and responding to the emotions it evokes in audiences even far from New Orleans, Terence Blanchard remarked, "When I travel, people ask me about my mom. I say, 'She's fine, thank you for asking.' But if you cried for my mom, you've got to multiply that amount of emotion by at least 100,000 people. Because that's how many people went through the exact same thing."[15] The individual experience of trauma, Blanchard implies, is intimately connected to an imagined collective experience, and it is this that both he and Spike Lee sought to capture and communicate, one through film and the other music. Audience reception of the kind that Blanchard speaks of here is one way to confirm the success of that communication.

Putting traumatic experience to music can have a therapeutic effect for an artist. Blanchard put the experience filmed by Lee to music as "Dear Mom," part of his Katrina requiem compact disc, *Tale of God's Will*. Blanchard recounts how he used the images provided in Lee's film as a basis from which to begin transforming emotions into music. "I was going on faith . . . Generally, when you do an album, you think about the songs, the tempos, the moods, how you can fit them into some kind of structure that makes sense and makes for an enjoyable listening experience. With this [Katrina experience], we didn't have a clue as to what it was going to be. We just needed to do it."[16] The images Blanchard worked from included those of his mother's reaction to seeing her destroyed home and his own filmed response. How does one represent such emotion when, as *Times-Picayune* music critic Keith Spera puts it, "words won't suffice"?[17] Blanchard found a way to express it through contrasting string instruments with his own trumpet playing. In Spera's words again, "As strings wrap around long, lush trumpet notes, the trumpeter salutes Wilhelmina Blanchard's courage and class, even as she mourns her tremendous loss."[18]

Words might not have sufficed in expressing the emotions wrought from viewing his family's grief, and the eerie mixing of strings and trumpet might have helped capture those feelings, but how does a musician communicate feeling to a distant audience? Can sound itself, with or without textual explanation or expression, communicate intense feeling of a specific nature? Blanchard's recording and the response it has engendered shows that it can, especially when performed in a context where Katrina is all-present. But what about when it is not, when the music is "just music"? Blanchard recognizes this issue and remarks that he sought to capture more universal feelings of suffering and loss in his Katrina requiem. His own involvement in the hurricane might have provided the emotional basis for his composition, but he hoped that personal feelings were transformed into something that could be grasped by others with no direct experience of Katrina who could nonetheless identify with the emotions contained in the music.

The intention to embed music with meaning is both confirmed and denied by another New Orleans musician practicing an entirely different genre, in which text complements sound. "The best thing about music is you can disappear in the moment," Paul Sanchez, a member of the New Orleans band Cowboy Mouth, told John Swenson,[19] as he described his first major post-Katrina public performance in January 2006. This would seem to deny what Blanchard intended. However, Sanchez also recounts the cathartic effect of that performance for musicians and audience. On such occasions, even old songs can take on a different meaning, and some, such as his band's staple number called "Hurricane Party," were difficult to perform. The song, written long before Katrina in response to Hurricane Andrew in 1992, contains the chorus, "Hurricane party, out of control / lying in the gutter eating Tootsie Rolls," and Sanchez says that during a road tour it became "almost impossible to play . . . I just couldn't do it."

"The kids like to throw Tootsie Rolls during that song, and those Tootsie Rolls landing on stage sounded like nails in my heart. I just couldn't sing the song, but the kids just kept holding up their New Orleans driver's license and calling for it. Finally we got home, and we were doing the reopening of the House of Blues show, and we put it back in. It was cathartic because that's the nature of live performance, but they were the most difficult shows I've ever played in my life."[20]

With reference to meaning, context might not be everything, but it is very significant. A song written in one context might well take on new meaning in another. The common thread in "Hurricane Party" is of course provided by the word "hurricane," but even without such a specific reference, an old song can take on new and powerful meaning in a highly charged context like a concert in the immediate aftermath of a traumatic occurrence. Bruce Springsteen's performance of "My City of Ruin," written about a New Jersey town, brought many to tears when performed at the first post-Katrina Jazz Fest in New Orleans in 2006, as it did when performed in New York after September 11, 2001. The Beatles song "Come Together" has nothing at all to do with New Orleans or hurricanes, but when performed at a post-Katrina festival it could bind a crowd in collective emotion. The song "New Orleans New Orleans" has nothing directly to do with hurricanes, but it became a rallying anthem for the city's recovery. More directly connected to flooding and disaster, but far removed in terms of time and context, Bessie Smith's blues standard "Backwater Blues" (in some minds, the first recorded blues song) could bring an audience to tears when sung by Irma Thomas, known locally as the queen of New Orleans R&B. In Thomas' slightly modified version, the line "When it thunders and lightnin' and the winds begin to blow/ thousands of people ain't got nowhere to go" could evoke powerful emotional identification in post-Katrina audiences. The song was recorded on the compilation album *Our New Orleans 2005*, along with performances by other New Orleans–based artists. Also included is an orchestrated version of Randy Newman's classic "Louisiana 1927," about another great flood that devastated the city. The song's compelling refrain "They're tryin' to wash us away" took on new meaning in a post-Katrina context filled with distrust and despair. One of New Orleans' most famous artists, Aaron Neville, has performed this song on numerous occasions, as has Newman himself. One can find a version on YouTube where Neville's voice is matched with images of the hurricane. The "they" referred to was part of an unspoken collective understanding, which would later be articulated in the phrase "Federal Flood" that is now used by local residents to describe Katrina.

It is thus difficult to specify which songs become authenticated representations of a traumatic occurrence, or which lyrics will evoke emotional response in those affected. One can say with more certainty that music, perhaps more than any other form of artistic expression, is an extremely powerful force in evoking and solidifying collective emotion. In merging sound and text, music binds minds and bodies, creating an aesthetic realm of individual and collective experience. Music can evoke identification and recognition, influencing the formation of collective identity; it can mobilize emotion, create mood, bind a group together, and provide solace, courage, hope, and, of course, escape.

As mentioned in the previous chapter, a *New Orleans Times-Picayune* reporter recounted that the spontaneous outburst of a gospel song by a woman stranded in front of the Superdome was his most powerful recollection of Katrina. Music has also provided a means for individual musicians to both express their anger and frustration and in some instances overcome their own trauma. Dr. John's CD *City That Care Forgot*, which received rave reviews from music critics when it was released in 2008, vented much anger toward those he felt were responsible for the social disaster that followed the storm. "I was angry from the beginning," the artist said. "My grief was very mixed with anger from the jump . . . there's so many things that have happened to people. It's really bad to me, how can so many things happen."[21] Dr. John, a former New Orleans resident, did not suffer directly from the storm, but another musician, jazz clarinetist Dr. Michael White, did. White lost family members and his entire musical collection to the floodwaters and fell into a deep depression. When finally able to enter a recording studio again, White recalled, "I didn't think I would be able to create anything at first," but listening to the music of others helped him through it and finally he was able to create his own music again:[22]

> What came first was a series of songs that were in a minor mode and that were very, very sad. I had been listening to a lot of things in a minor key, a lot of early gospel music, old spirituals . . . The song "Soon Will Be Gone The Troubles Of The World"—that song is so sad, I started playing that, and it seemed that a lot of stuff that I wrote was kind of in that mode, just sad and melancholy feelings. The cover photograph was of President Bush with the accompanying text, "Bush's Math, No Big Easy."[23]

The result was another "Katrina" recording, *Blue Crescent*, which also was well received by music critics. In explaining the importance of music in times of trouble, White remarked, "It's like the music regenerates itself. I didn't understand it then, but I very much understand it now. I felt like I channeled the music on *Blue Crescent* more than I composed it . . . It's all those experiences I've had in my life, through Katrina and into now. It's like all of that converted into music."[24] There is nothing political or accusatory in White's music; no one is named or blamed. In part, this is because instrumental music, especially when recorded, does not easily lend itself to politics in this manner. There are no words to say what is meant or felt, just the title and structured sounds. However, one does hear the sadness in the music and this is exactly what White felt and sought to convey. Dr. John's music is of an entirely different sort, and his intention here, as in the previously discussed *Voices of the Wetlands*, is clearly political. The anger he felt is vented in words as well as sounds; there is a clear message and addressee, as will be elaborated below.

The many benefit concerts and recordings after Katrina provided both funds for specific groups and emotional release for countless people. The question of which music, which sound, which text, is in a sense secondary to the power of the musical form itself, but it is a question that must be raised. While there may be no predicting exactly which music will arouse and bind individual and collective emotion after a traumatic occurrence, there are some common elements that can be uncovered. In the case of New Orleans and Katrina, there are specific musical traditions historically associated with the city and the region. These traditions, which have been termed "nostalgia music," can be heard and seen on any given day in the tourist quarters of New Orleans.[25] However, what is nostalgic in one context may be cathartic and mobilizing in another. Thus, "New Orleans New Orleans" or "When the Saints Go Marchin' In" may bring expressions of joy and recognition to crowds of tourists on one occasion, but may mobilize group resolution and purpose on another. In both cases, the specific sounds and texts call to mind a city and its musical traditions. One should distinguish here between the meaning that musical traditions or traditional music might have for tourists and what they might have for the musicians themselves. A young tuba player in a brass band second-line parade might find a different kind of rootedness in his performance than would the tourist watching from the sidelines. While the term "second line" is associated with funeral processions and brass bands, it carries musical meaning as well. According to Mac Rebennack, who later became better known as Dr. John and who grew up in this musical tradition, a second line is a "syncopated percussion beat . . . a 2/4 beat with double-time accents that can be played a million different ways."[26]

To sounds and musical traditions one could add generational and genre aspects. While elder tourists might closely identify and thus "hear" New Orleans in Dixieland or brass bands, those of a different age might find the same in Fats Domino's rollicking piano. The same could be applied to local variations of hip hop and punk, where different generations find collective identification within specific musical genres and with locally rooted variations within them. There are also words or phrases that evoke responses which suggest and channel meaning and interpretation. Thus, references to hurricanes or floods suggest individual and collective identification and association. Such identification can be expanded and deepened through phrases like "come together" or "coming home." Thirdly, artists performing particular musical pieces or particular artists themselves can evoke a specific response by adding on phrases, either in introducing a number or within the song itself. Thus, when performing a song like "Louisiana 1927," a performer might introduce the song by saying, "this has equal relevance today," or adding words like "FEMA's trying to wash us away."[27] Bruce Springsteen added new verses to his version of the blues classic "How Can a Poor Man Stand Such Times and Live" when he performed it at the New Orleans Jazz Fest in 2006. He introduced the song through reference to his previous day's experience in the Ninth Ward and other neighborhoods, where, he said, "I saw some sights I never thought I'd see in an American city. This is what happens when political cronyism guts the very agencies that are supposed to serve American citizens in times of trial and hardship."[28] Springsteen made his political intentions even more clear when he dedicated the song to "President Bystander," a clear reference to George W. Bush.

Some of the most powerful musical representations of Katrina are provided by hip hop artists such as Lil Wayne, who is from New Orleans, and Mos Def, who is not.[29] Lil Wayne (Dwayne Michael Carter, Jr.) was born in New Orleans in the predominantly African American Holly Grove neighborhood and made his first recording at the age of nine. Along with several other local artists, including Juvenile and B. G., he formed a group called the Hot Boys, which produced several top-selling recordings in the 1990s, along with successful solo efforts by individual members. Their music can be categorized as Gangsta rap. Lil Wayne's "Georgia Bush" is a good example of the sampling technique that turns a well-known lyric, in this case Ray Charles' "Georgia," into something entirely different. In the song, Charles' voice singing "Georgia" is quickly followed by Lil Wayne rapping

"Bush," so that one hears "Georgia Bush" through the combination. This is followed by powerful lyrics associating the American president with what is now accepted as the slow and feeble attempt at rescue and recovery. Lil Wayne's music has been used to make unofficial videos and has been distributed through YouTube and other means, and the combination of the song with images of the hurricane's devastation and political personages makes for very strong and emotionally compelling political commentary.

"Georgia Bush" represents Lil Wayne's entry into political discourse; in that sense, one could say that Katrina greatly affected his art. Yet it did not take long before he returned to the music and lifestyle that made him famous.[30] The song first appeared on a mixtape, a collection of songs made for public consumption, in 2006. Reviews of mixtapes sometimes appear in music magazines, widening their potential distribution beyond core audiences and local communities. "Dedication 2" was reviewed in major journals and newspapers around the country and was named in several of the year's top ten lists, including those of the *New York Times* and the *New Yorker*. Reviews and discussion circulated on the Internet, as did versions of the songs themselves. Jody Rosen of *Slate* called "Georgia Bush" "a real stunner . . . count on a New Orleans native to come up with the most eloquent, furious post-Katrina song yet" (http://www.slate.com/id/2150550/). Though not officially released and making use of illegal samples, "Dedication 2" and "Georgia Bush" were widely discussed and listened to.

In the opening line, Lil Wayne makes his addressee and his projected audience, the presumed "we," clear: "This song right here is dedicated to the President of the United States of America . . . This song is dedicated to the one wit the suit, Thick white skin and his eyes bright blue . . ."

Not only do the lyrics make clear who is responsible for the devastation caused by the hurricane, they also draw on the racial memory of past experience: one of the song's lines is "I know some folk that live by the levee / That keep telling me they heard the explosions." The reference to exploding the levees marks Lil Wayne as a New Orleans native who, though born in 1982, partakes of community-based memory from previous hurricanes. This rootedness in local traditions, however, does not produce any reflection concerning his own position in relation to that community or responsibility for it, except perhaps in the line "what is a survivor to do." Lil Wayne had left New Orleans before Katrina and was living in Houston when the hurricane struck. In fact, it is only the opening verses of "Georgia Bush" that address Katrina; the remaining verses return to Lil Wayne's more common themes of money and sex: "YEA! Money money money get a dollar and a dick" is the opening line of the third verse, and the rap continues in that vein for several more. Lil Wayne appears to be covering all his bases, offering powerful political commentary while at the same time making sure not to lose any of his core public. Nik Cohn goes so far as to call Katrina a "career boost" for Lil Wayne and other New Orleans rappers.[31] He writes, "knowing their core market was more excited by sex and money than social consciousness, they didn't overdo their grief, just let it be noted, and quickly got back to cheddar and hos."

Mos Def (Dante Terrell Smith), a Brooklyn-born and New York–based rapper and actor, recorded an equally compelling political commentary called "Dollar Day," better known by its original title, "Katrina Klap." We've already mentioned the song in the first chapter. The lyrics make clear who and what is responsible for the treatment of those left behind in the storm's wake:

> Listen, homie, it's Dollar Day in New Orleans
> It's water water everywhere and people dead in the streets
> And Mr. President he bout that cash
> He got a policy for handlin the niggaz and trash

The projected audience is clear from the opening line, "Listen, homie." "Homie" refers to those from the same area, as in "homeboy," a phrase popular among African American men at least since the 1960s. It generally refers to those from the same neighborhood or region of the country. In Mos Def's rap, the term makes the reference even broader by including all African Americans, even, one can speculate, women as well. As opposed to the "Gangsta"-rapping Lil Wayne, Mos Def treats women as something more than "hos and bitches." The lyrics aim at explaining that the government response to Hurricane Katrina was part of a wider policy with regard to poor blacks, if not African Americans generally. There is a pedagogy contained in the lyric, as the song is meant to inform as well as entertain, and when combined with visual imagery, as in the official video available for free on the Internet, it is a powerful tool of political education. Like catechism, rhyme and rhythm is easily absorbed, especially as both body and mind are involved. The final line of the verse, though ambiguous, points to a political practice: "Tell the boss, he shouldn't be boss anymore." What exactly this implies and who exactly is the "boss" is ambiguous, though one could infer something from the reference to "Mr. President."

Mos Def, who also uses the name Yasiin Bey, has played an active public role in the debate about politics and race in Katrina's aftermath. Videos of his post-Katrina trips to New Orleans are available on the Internet and are full of political commentary about the causes of the hurricane and the role of race in the official response. The artist makes clear his own position in an interview in the opening sequence in one of these videos: "I don't feel comfortable with my success . . . I'm a nobody in relation to this shit. And if I don't use the power that I've been given in the world to address this shit I might as well just go lay in the casket. Just go lay down."[32] "Shit" presumably refers to the treatment of blacks in Katrina's aftermath. In another interview,[33] after being guided around the city by local activists, Mos Def declares that he is not an activist in the direct sense of the term; he is "just doin' what one should," defending oneself against the "bullshit," which he later goes on to describe as the "casual systemic indifference to black life." For this rapper, Katrina is a metaphor for this systemic indifference, one that had a powerful impact on his approach to art.

The previously mentioned Dr. John and his CD *City That Care Forgot*, released in 2008, should be analyzed in relation to these rap artists. Dr. John, or Mac Rebennack, was born in New Orleans' Third Ward, but left to live in Los Angeles long before Katrina struck. Yet he clearly identifies with the city, and his music, a mixture of funk, rhythm and blues, and old time piano, is identified by many as New Orleans music. The subtitle of the CD *City That Care Forgot* is *Lower 911*, which emphasizes the political nature of its contents through a double reference. The numbers 911 have been etched into world consciousness as symbolizing the September 11, 2001, attacks on New York's World Trade Center. Remembered and commemorated in the United States as one of the worst attacks against the American nation, the implicit comparison made between these attacks and Katrina is to raise the meaning of the latter to the highest level. The second embedded meaning in 911 is that it recalls the emergency number used throughout the country, which one dials in extreme need. At least with regard to its impact on one New Orleans neighborhood, the Lower Ninth Ward, Katrina can be compared to the attack on the World Trade Center, and Dr. John is making the emergency call for help. Who is to blame and who is being called to help? The song texts, some of which are based on newspaper columns by Chris Rose, tell us plainly. I will focus on two, "Dream Warrior" and "Say Whut?" "Dream Warrior" is a battle cry for a citizen's revolt against the perceived injustices wrought in Katrina's wake. After declaring his status as a rebel warrior, Dr. John recalls and proclaims his Louisiana roots and identification, along with his struggles to save the wetlands:

I'm a samurai of the holy lost cause
Of the river and the bayou and the fishin holes
Louisiana born, Louisiana brave

Then the chorus names the perpetrators and the victims:

> If you don't understand, lemme explain
> About the second battle of New Orleans
> Not about the loss, not even the devastation
> About it was done with intention
> Dark and spoiled when they blew that levee

The reference to blowing the levee is ambiguous. It could be to the 1927 flood, when the levees of the Mississippi were dynamited and the river diverted to save wealthy white parts of the city at the expense of the poorer and blacker neighborhoods. It could also be to the belief, held by some African Americans, that something similar was done again during Katrina. More important perhaps is the phrase "done with intention," the implication that there were conscious decisions made during the flooding that favored some groups of the population at the expense of others. Reference is also made to CNN, most likely a stand-in for all the mainstream media, which were the object of disdain for many locals who perceived bias in their coverage and reporting.

The lyrics of "Say Whut?" are even more explicit and compelling. Though not directly named, President Bush comes in for blunt and sarcastic criticism for his support of FEMA director Michael Brown and his seeming aloofness toward those who suffered.

> Mamas cryin', babies dyin'
> And you call that good
> Say it's a job well done
> Then you giggled like a bitch
> Hopped back on Air Force 1

Those deemed responsible for the fate of Katrina's victims are announced loud and clear.

Katrina united three artists with audiences that otherwise would have had little to do with one another. Though their music can be loosely classified as rap, Lil Wayne and Mos Def have little in common and the same can be said for their respective audiences. Lil Wayne's Gangsta performance style and the added New Orleans bounce of his music is different from Mos Def's more straightforward presentation, where, as in folk music, the lyric and the message it contains take on greater importance. Mos Def had an already well-established reputation and the requisite audience as a politically engaged performer when he made "Katrina Klap." Lil Wayne, on the other hand, temporarily stepped outside his audience to make "Georgia Bush," and then stepped as quickly back in. Those who find Dr. John's music appealing would not likely be enthusiastic rap fans and would probably never have listened to either Lil Wayne or Mos Def had it not been for Katrina and New Orleans.[34]

FOR INTERPRETATION

In any contemporary aesthetic response to tragedy and trauma, there is always the danger of exploitation and insincerity stemming largely from commercial interest. As one New Orleans musician put it when asked about his role in the restoration of the city, "I'm just doing my little part of bringing some attention to a place that was beautiful and special. It's not like these are songs that are linked to an event. Often these things come out not sounding so genuine . . . I know their intentions are good. But it's dangerous territory."[35] Artists have to make a living, and the tension between empathy, aesthetics, and commercial interest is always present. Aesthetic representation in response to a traumatic occurrence only intensifies this tension. Representing the pain of others, as Susan Sontag has written, contains an inherent danger of voyeurism and exploitation, as well as aestheticizing—making suffering appear pleasing to the eye or ear.[36] Adorno implied the same when he proclaimed that aesthetic silence might be preferable to writing poetry after Auschwitz. Artists and musicians like those discussed so far have taken care to control as much as possible the meaning derived from their work. Once a poem is written, however, or a picture made, or a song released, the creator loses control over its interpretation and the uses a work of art might be put to. How much control over meaning and interpretation an artist has varies to some degree with genre. While a photograph or a painting do not speak for themselves and require a viewer to complete their meaning, they do objectify, framing an incident or a person as a totality that can be grasped and possessed. Even photographs, which make more of a claim to objectivity and truth than music or painting, are always selective; they reflect the view and vision of the photographer, placing the viewer "in the same position as the lackey behind the camera," as Sontag so pointedly puts it.[37] What position does a piece of music put the listener in and what reactions does it arouse? Mos Def would like his audiences to react emotionally and politically, but what does Lil Wayne expect from his audience? Both have infused these songs with political meaning but cannot know with any certainty how they will be interpreted and received. In part, this stems from the fact that audiences, even for genre music like rap, are multilayered and shifting—which perhaps explains why Lil Wayne made sure to include something for his core public, one more interested in sex and money than political commentary. A general point, however, is that there is no necessary connection between embedded meaning—what an artist intends to evoke, if there is any such intention—and how that work will be interpreted. The context of interpretation is an important factor in effect and meaning. Political rap like these two examples, which clearly intend to affect how one understands Hurricane Katrina, is more likely to have that "preferred reading" in a context where the event is being remembered and/or where those gathered have some direct interest in or experience of the event.[38] These can be survivors, sympathizers, and political activists in general—even more generally, African Americans—once the hurricane has been racialized and associated with the broad issue of race in American society. Those outside these categories might hear only noise. And, as discussed above, the context in which these songs are performed plays a very important role in how they will be interpreted.

It need not be emphasized that music is a central part of what New Orleans means and represents. One of the most threatened aspects of this collective identity after Katrina is the local traditions rooted in various ethnic neighborhoods. The most obvious of these are the brass bands and the funeral marches, and the second-line parades that are their most public expression.[39] The brass bands have a direct connection to poorer African American neighborhoods, like Treme in the Sixth Ward, Gentilly, and the Lower Ninth Ward.[40] Two social factors have combined to alter these neighborhoods and threaten their musical traditions in the post-Katrina recovery. The first is age. Many of those who died in the flood and suffered most in its aftermath were older residents, some of whom were important carriers of older musical traditions. Swenson recounts a number of their stories.[41] As these older musicians die or move away, a significant part of New Orleans music dies with them. A second factor concerns other demographic factors, such as race and income and the interests related to them. As statistics presented earlier suggest, the return rates to poorer neighborhoods are significantly lower than to wealthier ones, and here race factors in. The neighborhood with the lowest rate of return, the Lower Ninth Ward, was also a neighborhood rich in musical traditions, with brass bands and second-line parades, as well as Mardi Gras Indians. For many analysts, these musical styles form the core of New Orleans music. As they are the ones most rooted in neighborhood traditions, they are the most threatened by shifting demographics. Gentrification requires consideration; shifting demographic patterns have hastened the process of gentrification in certain formerly African American neighborhoods like Treme, a process that will likely have an effect on musical tastes and traditions. As young whites move in, the older rituals like funeral marches and second lines that nourished the brass bands are likely to be affected, though of course new musical fusions might evolve.

One effect of Katrina on the New Orleans music scene and perhaps on New Orleans music in general is that in thinning out many of the neighborhoods traditionally populated by African Americans, such as the Lower Ninth Ward, and in shaking up the old neighborhoods, it may have started a shift in the social basis of the city's music. Swenson points to such a development, suggesting that musical affinity rather than ethnicity is now the grounds of musical cooperation: "With the shuffled populace changing the city's demographics, new neighborhood alliances were forming. Mardi Gras Indian music and brass-band culture had been almost exclusively African American before the storm, but in its wake musicians were cooperating based more on musical affinity than ethnicity."[42]

THE VISUAL ARTS

Representing disaster and trauma through the visual arts has been a topic of reflection for centuries. Edmund Burke and Immanuel Kant developed the concept of the sublime to understand the power of nature or human tragedy to inspire awe, thus expanding the idea and range of the beautiful from classical traditions. According to Aric Mayer,[43] a photographer who covered Katrina for the *Wall Street Journal*, there are two basic aesthetic positions from which one can depict natural disasters. The first is documentary realism, "which works to focus on the humanitarian issues to evoke a kind of empathy in the viewer by depicting suffering and deprivation." The second approach "works on landscape to point to the scale of the destruction in an effort to generate an experience of the breadth of the event."[44] One could add that while documentary realism attempts to draw the viewer closer to what is being depicted, the aesthetic focus creates distance. Sontag unifies these in what she calls the "dual powers of photography—to generate documents and to create works of visual art."[45] Documentary realism is the stance that guided most of the photojournalism discussed in a previous chapter, where photographers sought to document what they saw and also, in conjunction with editorial writers, to bring their readers closer to the subjects they depicted. In this regard, Mayer makes some interesting observations regarding the impact of size and format. Newspapers print photographs in limited size and quantity, something which also limits their impact. Mayer wanted more, so he began composing a set of larger photographs designed with gallery exhibition rather than newspaper publication in mind. He writes, "I composed the images in a format specifically to be printed between thirty and sixty inches square, a scale at which the photographs start to interact with the viewer in a more powerful way than do the much smaller scale images that are routinely circulated through photojournalism."[46] While the smaller photographs were intended to create empathy and to mobilize opinion, the larger were meant to be aesthetically pleasing. The danger in the latter is that they risk making devastation and death into something beautiful. As Sontag puts it, "the landscape of devastation is still a landscape."[47] While Sontag goes on to point out that photographs transform their subjects into something palatable, if not necessarily beautiful, the dangers inherent in the aesthetic representation of suffering are present in all visual representation, but perhaps more so in painting than photography. Mayer's photographs appeared in the *Wall Street Journal* and were also exhibited in the city as part of the first anniversary commemoration.[48] He argues for an alternative representation, which he then tries to illustrate through his own photos. That alternative consists in attempting to represent what Kant and others thought was unrepresentable, namely, the massiveness and the totality of the disaster, seen as a natural disaster.

How does one represent the power of nature in a culture where nature has become landscape, or what Horkheimer and Adorno (1972) called "second nature," by which they meant a tamed and colonized outdoors? One way, Mayer argues, is through the scale: large-sized photos, rather than small ones that tend to create an intimacy between the photo and the viewer. Another way is to present images that represent the totality, the city rather than people, with wide-angle and distant perspectives that include the sky and the water as well as the destroyed made objects. Mayer says he is not out to deny the value of these two perspectives, for each has its time and function. Documentary realism was important in the early stages of Katrina in creating empathy with the victims and helping to mobilize sympathy and resources; it moves people to feel and to act in the best case, and this is what happened in Katrina. However, this perspective, he says, has diminishing returns, in that once aid is given the public turns to other things. Or worse, they may simply turn off emotionally and say, "we've seen enough."

Once the immediate and pressing needs of the survivors were addressed, more complicated and troubling questions began to emerge. How could a rich and advanced country like the United States leave its citizens in the center of a disaster for nearly a week without relief? This question and the many political, social, and racial issues that it raises are hardly addressed in any meaningful way in the photojournalistic images, the primary source of visual understanding of Katrina for the nation.[49]

These tensions were reflected upon by the New Orleans–based artist Phil Sandusky as he and a colleague moved around the city directly after the storm in search of suitable subjects, what they termed "virgin, natural destruction."[50] After painting devastated homes in neighborhoods near his own (his house suffered minimal damage), Sandusky moved to a nearby yacht club where

> . . . there were no broken lives, or at least there didn't seem to be, just multitudes of broken boats. And they were beautiful! We could now say things to each other such as, "Wow, man, look at this—this is really neat," without feeling as though we were desecrating a grave. Perhaps the guilt I had been experiencing in the neighborhoods all along was because deep down I had felt, as I did in the yacht basin, like a kid in a candy shop. Artistically these things we saw were so beautiful.[51]

The tension between the aesthetic vantage point that can find beauty in devastation and suffering and the human capacity for empathy was later resolved. "By the time we received word that certain parts of the Lower Ninth Ward were being opened to the public, I had resolved the internal conflicts between my artistic motives and the need to demonstrate my sadness for all the pain and misery Katrina had inflicted on my beloved city. It would be OK to feel artistically elated on the inside, as long as it was coupled with quiet respect."[52] At the same time, Sandusky acknowledges that his paintings "were more emotionally charged, knowing that so many people died" in the neighborhoods he painted.[53] If the painter's emotional engagement with his subject was tension-filled, so were his motivations, though these were not as explicitly acknowledged. On the one hand, there was "the desire to document," to bear witness to the devastation, something which Sandusky is very clear about. On the other hand, there was the unspoken knowledge that these paintings have potential commercial value, especially for a well-established artist like himself. The hurricane provided this artist with new subjects and an opportunity and stimulation to paint; the fact that he was personally affected, that this was his "beloved city," was overridden or perhaps even abetted by this emotional attachment, by aesthetic desire. Other artists would do the same; New Orleans painter Terrance Osborne painted colorful floating houses, as mentioned in the opening chapter, and musician–turned–street artist M. D. Haberdasher sold old photographs laminated onto cut remnants of his Treme house.

Like the tension between guilt and awe at the aesthetic qualities of death and destruction, the tension between the desire to bear witness and the potential commercial value of a work of art can be resolved by suppressing the latter as one is moved and motivated by the former. The artist does not need to think about commerce in the midst of the moment of aesthetic desire. The same is true for the viewer of these paintings. Especially when collected in a book and viewed long after the storm, Sandusky's paintings can be experienced as beautiful representations of wreckage, without any emotion beyond the aesthetic appreciation of the skilled representation of color and form. Even as presented in this published form, with paintings of New Orleans houses and streets before and after Katrina, there is no real sense of pain or loss necessarily contained in these paintings. They are works of art that could have been painted anywhere. It is the quality of the work, aesthetic considerations, that dominate, not any embedded meaning. The subject in fact is objectified, beautiful ruins finely composed and rendered. Katrina is a storm, not a symbol. However, for those directly involved, these are not just paintings, and the objects they represent are not neutral or beautiful in any way. "There is nothing beautiful here," said one neighborhood resident to Sandusky in response to the painter's claim to find beauty in the devastation.[54]

An even more distant, though not more detached, approach to the aftermath of Katrina can be found in works by the Dallas-based artist David Bates. Bates produced a suite of paintings exhibited at several venues under the title *The Katrina Paintings* and published in a book with the same title. Bates began making sketches as he watched the hurricane unfold on television from his home in Texas.[55] In contrast to Sandusky's hands-on approach, Bates is more interested in people than architecture, though this collection does include works of wrecked houses and flooded landscapes, apparently painted from photographs. Even here, though, one gets the impression that houses are homes, and though their inhabitants are not always pictured, people once lived in them. Human anguish and suffering appears to be Bates' direct concern, even if the people he paints are images taken from a television screen. Nearly all the faces and figures are of African Americans and are filled with anguish and despair. The source of this despair is clear from the surrounding wreckage, but the object of their anger is not. As with Sandusky's work, the issue of responsibility is not directly addressed, except perhaps in terms of the artist to his subject. No political commentary is provided, and though an accusatory finger does make an appearance in several portraits, it is not pointed in any specific direction, except perhaps at the viewer.

Bates' Katrina paintings have been compared to the documentary photography of Depression-era America by Dorothea Lange and Walker Evans and to more contemporary political portraiture by Robert Shetterly.[56] Like Lange and Evans, Bates provides no answer to the question of who is responsible for the suffering depicted, and unlike Shetterly, he provides no textual commentary to make that clear. Like Terence Blanchard's quietly moaning trumpet, Bates' paintings create a somber mood and leave the question of interpretation to the viewer. Yet his survivors are not passive victims; their faces are angry and defiant. While the object of that anger is not clearly spelled out, the emotion is apparent and real. One senses that these people know who is responsible and that you should too. This is different from Lange and Evans, who set out to bear witness rather than to comment, and different from Shetterly, who comments more than he witnesses. The portraits also turn the issue of responsibility back on the viewer. All are painted in direct face-to-face confrontation with the viewer. Little writes of Bates, "In paying homage to the survivors of Hurricane Katrina, to their sorrow and pain, he reminds us of our humanity. Turning his gaze outward, Bates bears witness to tragedy even as he illuminates who we are as human beings."[57] The question, though, concerns the content of that humanity and what, if any, responsibility to others it entails. Bates' confrontational faces seem to be asking us to ponder what we are looking at and what we intend to do about it.

Sandusky makes an interesting observation on the difference between painting and photography as witness to disaster. Photographers, he writes, are

> . . . in the enviable position of being able to dart into a place they are not supposed to be, shoot a couple of rolls of film, and get out. Being a plein-air painter, it takes me hours to set-up and do one painting. This makes me more vulnerable to the authorities. Also, I must choose my subjects more carefully. I will have so few paintings to say what needs to be said about all of this.[58]

We will discuss some of the photographers who documented Katrina shortly, but it is worth first pondering what it is that Sandusky means by "what needs to be said about all of this." Does he mean aesthetically, or perhaps morally? If these are the options, Sandusky has clearly opted for the first; he makes no moral or political judgments. There are no accusatory fingers pointing at the viewer; there are no fingers or hands at all. It is a natural disaster that is documented here, and what needs to be said is that from the aesthetic point of view nature can be beautiful in its destructiveness. Bates, on the other hand, says something quite different with his paintings. What "needs to be said" about Katrina is that it may have begun as a natural disaster but it ended as a social catastrophe, and the artist has the responsibility to represent that, to reveal how the forces of nature impacted human beings—and also just who those human beings were. While both artists exhibited and sold their works in galleries, the impact on the viewer, one can surmise, was intended to be different: Sandusky awes, and pleases the viewer with his skill in rendering and revealing the aesthetic dimensions of disaster. Bates confronts the viewer, evoking discomfort rather than pleasure.

The various works of art contained in the collection *Sustained Winds* (2006) reflect some of these tensions and different approaches to representing disaster and trauma. The works were exhibited at the Acadiana Center for the Arts in Lafayette, Louisiana. On the cover of the exhibition's catalogue and featured in the show is a triptych by Dona Simons entitled *Evolution of Evangeline*, which records on its surface the damage done to the original *Evangeline* triptych, which was damaged by flood waters. The painting features a single female figure standing in front of a cornfield. In the first rendition, the body is finely formed, with skin smooth and clear; light brown hair flows in the natural light. As the viewer moves to the second and third paintings, the figure's hair has turned a watery blue tint, the skin is no longer smooth, and the face has turned a deathly pale. The figures represent Evangeline before, during, and after Katrina, a format that became familiar in the post-Katrina visual arts. There is no clear political intention here, but the composition and its placement in an exhibition of post-Katrina art is both emotional and evocative, and could be experienced as political art when seen alongside other more directly political works. The viewer is asked to grieve for the sorrowful Evangeline, a name which itself evokes identification in this region of the country. The grief and sense of loss evoked by this triptych contrasts with another work from the same exhibition, the explicitly political *Negligent Homicide* by David Holcombe. This is a combined portrait of three figures, Salvador Mangano, Mabel Mangano, and Ray Nagin, as criminals. Nagin of course is the former mayor of New Orleans, and the Manganos are identified as the owners of a nursing home where, we are told, thirty-four residents died in the flooding. Mayor Nagin is accused of being responsible for the deaths of eight hundred city residents. Another triptych, by Grace Liberator, called *Katrina and the days that followed I, II, III*, portrays African American suffering and caring in portraits of parents and children. Also included are items of found and assembled art, such as the now heavily symbolic refrigerators by Tom Varisco, decorated with tape and words like "Spoiled" and "R.I.P." There are many paintings and photographs of wreckage, destruction, and dead animals in this exhibition.

A major exhibition with the name Prospect.1 New Orleans, featuring eighty-one artists from thirty-nine countries, was scattered around twenty-three locations in New Orleans beginning in November 2008. Organized by the visual arts curator of the New Orleans Contemporary Art Center (CAC), the idea behind this exhibition was to help uplift the city through an international exhibition along the lines of the Venice Biennale. The exhibition inspired, though it did not sponsor, various forms of street art, such as the found-art "reclamations" by local artist and gallery owner Christopher Porche West, who assembled pieces of post-Katrina rubble into a large pile in front of his gallery. These were forcibly removed by the police.[59] One of the participating artists in Prospect.1 was Takashi Horisaki, a Japanese national who studied at Loyola University and considered New Orleans his American home (interviewed on www.arts.gov/artworks?cat=123). Horisaki had moved to New York by the time Katrina hit, but he was inspired to return by the televised images of destruction. The result of this visit was an installation entitled *Social Dress New Orleans—730 Days After*, which consists of a latex-skin form of a house suspended on ropes to form a whole. The work was first exhibited in New York and then transported by the artist in a van to New Orleans for Prospect.1. The actual house at 1941 Caffin Avenue in the Lower Ninth Ward was about to be demolished by the city when Horisaki asked for a reprieve to complete his work.[60] That he found himself in the Ninth Ward in the wake of the storm was only part happenstance. In New Orleans to view the damage and visit friends, Horisaki found himself and his art object in one of the most devastated neighborhoods of the city. This all followed from his view that art and the artist should be rooted in a community and be an inspiration to its members:

> When I decided to do this project, at first I kept feeling guilty about making an art piece because I didn't think I would be helping anyone out since I was not gutting and rebuilding houses . . . Instead I found myself in what appeared to be the middle of nowhere in the ninth ward, painting what seemed to be gray paint on a clearly unlivable house.[61]

Guilt gave way to creative enthusiasm as passersby encouraged him to continue. Horisaki found his purpose and inspiration: "To me, such inspiration—both the hope of the locals and the action of those outside the immediate community—are really the most invaluable effects of a good art piece, and it is what I aspire to in all my projects."[62] Prior to coming to New Orleans and beginning this work, Horisaki had finished an installation entitled *Social Dress Buffalo*, an homage to another threatened American city.

A moving document of post-Katrina New Orleans is *Floodwall*, a multimedia installation created by New Orleans resident Jana Napoli (www .floodwall.org). Like Horisaki's work, *Floodwall* was first exhibited in New York City, within sight of Ground Zero, before traveling to the Louisiana State Museum in Baton Rouge. The New York placement of the work drew attention to the connection between two American traumas.[63] *Floodwall* is an installation organized around a "wall" composed of hundreds of empty dresser drawers that Napoli collected from post-Katrina debris. Each drawer is inscribed with the address from where it was taken, offering the same type of authenticity as Horisaki's work. Napoli's work is also inspired by hope. In this case, the hope is to reconnect with the actual owner and collect the stories associated with these personal possessions. Napoli and her collaborators have created a website for this purpose, hoping that those who once owned these drawers will see the exhibition as it travels across the country. This is a new and creative use of the Internet, linking artwork and website as forms of communication and discovery. In a sense, the Internet here replaces the poster board or reading wall where refugees once posted messages in town squares across war-torn Europe. Similar "walls" have sprung up in spontaneous memorials following other disasters, including 9/11.

In the *Floodwall* installation, the seven hundred drawers are arranged as a wall, perhaps a wailing wall as well as a floodwall, with the intention of giving voice to "all those families left behind."[64] They were left behind, Napoli says, "because we just were not American enough for the rest of America." Napoli herself sat out Katrina in her home in Metairie, just outside New Orleans, unable to leave at first because of her ninety-year-old mother, who was ill with dementia. It was a situation similar to those of many who "chose" to remain behind and ride out the storm. According to Napoli, the role of the artist is "to make images for the things people do not yet have words for."[65] In the case of Katrina, this meant two things: giving voice to those whose lives were destroyed, and representing in material form the eerie silence experienced by everyone who returned to New Orleans soon after the storm. The installation is also meant to "speak for my city." Collecting these drawers and turning them into mementos to disrupted lives meant more than giving voice to others. Napoli says that "saving the drawers saved me . . . helped me burn up my grief and anger" at being "not American enough for the rest of America." *Floodwall* articulated and communicated the artist's personal trauma as well as that of the collectivity that was New Orleans.

In an insightful analysis, Joy Fuqua sets *Floodwall* in the context of 9/11 and national trauma, bringing yet another dimension of trauma to the work.[66] The fact that *Floodwall* was first exhibited at a location within sight of the former World Trade Center in Manhattan makes the comparison seem natural: "Napoli's piece invites us to draw together two national traumas that are often held apart."[67] While both may be analyzed as national traumas, there are significant differences in potentiality. While the 9/11 attacks on the United States occurred in a recognized national center, Katrina, Fuqua writes, occurred on the national periphery, a point echoed by many, including Jana Napoli: "New Orleans has always figured as a place with tenuous claims to 'American-ness.'"[68] This difference, Fuqua contends, was reflected in the media coverage of the two incidents, with 9/11 being covered without commercial interruption, while Katrina was not. More significant perhaps was the actual context of the coverage and how 9/11 was "immediately embraced as a national tragedy; a variety of institutional and governmental entities used it to stoke the flames of nationalism and so-called pre-emptive war as the preferred response, crafting a narrative of patriotism and national allegiance replete with demarcated heroes and villains."[69] Katrina, on the other hand, was discussed in terms of race and poverty, as has been shown in the previous chapter. Katrina was a "national shame" with victims who could be blamed for their victimhood and with no clear heroes or villains, a "discursive frame [which] prevents the type of national embrace . . . that New York has received."[70]

In its attempt to represent trauma, individual and collective, through personal objects, *Floodwall* reminds one also of various Holocaust memorials, where the goods left behind by victims are arranged for display. One significant difference, however, is that the artist has here the intention of reaching these victims, in the hope they are alive and well. In fact, part of the multimedia arrangements in this installation is the recorded voices of those owners of drawers who have been identified and who are willing to tell their Katrina story. Something similar has been done in Holocaust memorials, like the one on the Mall in Washington, DC, where one is given a name of a victim and can trace his or her fate as one passes through the museum.

Found objects, remnants of a lived past before the storm, are also on display at a memorial site in Biloxi, Mississippi, a coastal city devastated by Katrina, part of which is "a clear Plexiglas box filled with found and donated objects—shoes, dolls, a flag, pieces of clothing, a cross, a clock."[71]

This memorial was donated by the people behind the reality television show *Extreme Makeover Home Edition*, a fact that Natasha Trethewey, an American poet laureate, finds disturbing. "The memorial not only remembers the storm and the people but also inscribes on the landscape a narrative of the commercialization of memory."[72] While governments may build memorials that promote feelings of collective belonging which can be exploited, so too, suggests Trethewey, can corporations create memorials with the aim of promoting their own interests. Where we can more easily uncover the meaning of memorials for governments, what is the meaning of Katrina for such corporations? What did they want to express with their sponsorship? From the perspective laid out by Fuqua,[73] and more generally by Negra,[74] it may well be to help contain the meaning of Katrina within the bounds of established ideas and myths about the American way of life as currently interpreted.

In her Introduction to the edited volume within which Fuqua's chapter appears, Negra writes: "Representations of Hurricane Katrina cannot be read outside of a neoliberal context marked by 'New Economy' market fundamentalism, state-sponsored assaults on the environment, intense anti-immigration rhetoric in a nation that still celebrates itself as a global beacon of hope for the downtrodden, the withering role of state care for the vulnerable . . ."[75] Trethewey would agree, but presents her case in a more veiled manner, the language of a poet perhaps. In her reminiscing of the meaning of Katrina for the Mississippi Gulf coast, she obliquely criticizes new Mississippi laws permitting onshore casinos to flourish where there once were homes and communities for less well-off inhabitants. The new commercially inspired residents, she makes clear, will directly threaten the ecological balance of the region: "the future of the Mississippi Gulf Coast's environment is tied to the stability of the wetlands, the possibility of rising tide levels—due, in part, to global warming rates—and the potential impact of humans and development along the coast."[76] This "development" follows directly from legislation favoring commercial interests, building casinos instead of low-income housing for those who lived there prior to Katrina. Like Napoli and Horisaki, Trethewey speaks to and for these people in her post-Katrina poem "Liturgy":

> To Miss Mary, somewhere
> To the displaced, living in trailers along the coast,
> beside the highway,
> in vacant lots and open fields, to everyone who stayed
> on the coast,
> who came back—or cannot—to the coast;

To those who died on the coast.
This is a memory of the coast: to each his own
recollections, her recollections, their
recollections, the return of the coast.
This is a time capsule for the coast: words of the people
—don't forget us—

For Trethewey, the Gulf coast of her youth and her family history, which she traces in *Beyond Katrina*, will never be what it was—time, and hurricanes, move people on. But time and hurricanes, she makes clear, have help from politicians and other powerful interests. Katrina revealed this truth one more time.

The New Orleans poet Brad Bechler is also concerned with memory and forgetting in the volume of poetry he published to commemorate the storm's fourth anniversary.[77] His book, *When Will the Sky Fall*, carries the subtitle *Hurricane Katrina, a Documentary in Poetry*. The poems are meant to keep memory alive through word-images that evoke emotional responses. With titles like "Three Years Later," "Katrina Relief?" and "Attic," Bechler would like to sear Katrina into American memory. We will return to the issue of memory and the representation of trauma (and to Brad Bechler) in the final chapter.

PHOTOGRAPHY

There are many collections of photographs of the devastation and suffering caused by Katrina. One of the most powerful follows the format of the previously discussed book by the artist Phil Sandusky, with selections of photographers' work before, during, and after the hurricane. Here the intention is to reveal how the hurricane impacted the photographers and affected their aesthetic approach. The exhibition *Before (During) After* included the work of twelve photographers who lived through the storm.[78] It is not clear whether or not these photographers darted in and out of the damaged area in order to take their pictures. Like Sandusky, all lost something during the storm, and a few lost nearly everything. What they depict, then, has more than aesthetic meaning to them, as they were personally affected by the hurricane, making its devastation not simply an object of interest, but an experience filled with subjective emotion. This emotional connection is made immediately apparent by showing the contrast in how they worked before and after Katrina. Working a bit in the style of Sandusky, but using a camera instead of a brush, Frank Relle was interested in representing what he termed the rich culture of New Orleans through its architecture. He too was moved by what he saw in Katrina's aftermath. He writes,

> While each house I photograph has something different to show me, one overriding lesson I have learned is to get out there and get the picture, no matter what. If I contemplated photographic concepts before going out into the barricaded Ninth Ward at night, I don't think I would have made these photographs. I never asked for permission. Instead, I asked for forgiveness.[79]

The same tension appears in Relle's relation to his representations of devastation: the realization that what might make interesting subject matter for a photographer comes at great cost in human suffering. Yet the impulse to record is too strong to resist. In both the painter and the photographer, one finds a similar interest. The houses of the city are their subjects, both before and after the storm, and the unease comes from what these houses might mean for those who live in them, though in both cases these are absent subjects. In terms of what they represent, there appears to be little difference between the paintings and the photographs. The medium is not the message.

A powerful firsthand account of the impact of the hurricane is offered by David Spielman,[80] a New Orleans photographer and gallery owner who remained in the city during the storm and after. The fact the Spielman includes his diary notes recounting his reflections, observations, and activities makes his account appear all the more authentic. Having decided to remain in his home in the predominantly white Uptown section of the city, "on some of the highest ground around," Spielman is quite candid about his initial intentions. "I was coming to the conclusion that Katrina was not going to offer me any worthwhile images. I am a freelance photographer and not being a hard news guy, I hadn't seen anything so far that was going to win any awards."[81] Spielman moved from his own home to a nearby Catholic convent, which was housed in a solid brick building and where he was old friends with the resident nuns. As the storm passed, he toured the passable parts of the city in his running shoes, at this point unaware that the levees had been damaged and the flooding had begun. This changed on Tuesday, August 30, as the water rose and spread throughout the city. Spielman reports hearing gunshots on St. Charles Avenue, one of the central thoroughfares connecting Uptown to downtown, and seeing "young men scouting" as he jogged that day. "The lack of police protection was also noticed and mentioned by most of the people I spoke with."[82] While inspecting his gallery, Spielman reports chasing looters away with a gun he had brought with him. He later photographed looters at a local Walmart, recounting that New Orleans police officers stood idly by. Reporting these occurrences to the authorities at the convent led to their decision to evacuate the city. Spielman remained behind alone in the enormous building without power, water, or any means of communication. At his gallery, he discovered that the landline telephone was working, and by removing the phone and plugging his computer into the jack Spielman was able to send e-mail messages to the rest of the world. The commentaries contained in the book are the daily e-mails he sent out. Spielman's dramatic photographs, depicting the devastation in many parts of the city, and his daily commentary of the situation on the ground make for compelling documentary, an eyewitness account from the perspective of a resident and professional photographer. There appears to be a conscious effort to balance what is represented; in one place, on opposing pages, he presents an image of a mansion on Audubon Place damaged by fire and a severely damaged shotgun house in the Ninth Ward. There are more photographs of National Guard soldiers than of survivors seeking help and none of obvious criminality. Spielman points no fingers and places no blame. His Katrina story is one of survival, resilience, and resourcefulness under extreme conditions.

As with music, the context, the time and place, in which these works of visual art are viewed is of great importance. The viewer's perspective and relationship, if any, to the hurricane and the region are also important. Artworks are most often displayed in galleries and museums and are presented in particular ways. The artist has an interest in presenting a body of work, the gallery owner is interested in making a sale, and the museum curator has a range of interests. The works are arranged and selected by professionals, with a specific aim, just as was the *Katrina and Beyond* exhibition at the Louisiana State Museum. These aims are as much a part of the "preferred reading" as the intentions of the creator in producing the work. The examples so far discussed were rendered as artworks, though their creators had various other intentions as well—for example, documenting and witnessing. The exhibition at the Louisiana State Museum was not an art exhibition, though it did display objects that would be considered artworks in another context as well as objects which became artworks through their appearance at this exhibition. A door from a destroyed home with a spray-painted X on it to indicate that it had been searched for dead bodies becomes an aesthetic object, if not a work of art, when displayed together with "authentic" works of art. Especially when presented together with a photograph of the object's maker, these items tell a story in an aesthetically conditioned context. This contextualization influences the way they are viewed and understood. They could be called "ready-mades." Like Duchamp's urinal or Warhol's soup cans, they become artworks when displayed in a particular environment, but unlike them, they are not expected to evoke the question, "is this art?" Rather, the intention is to evoke reflection on how "this" came to be. How did it happen that a refrigerator with rotting food inside is displayed here? Who and what is responsible for someone being stuck in an attic for nearly a week?

THE POPULAR ARTS

Katrina made appearances in popular literature, theater, documentary film, and television. James Lee Burke, a popular and prolific crime writer, added Katrina as a setting for his Louisiana-based police detective Dave Robicheaux in *The Tin Roof Blowdown*.[83] In setting the scene for a criminal case involving the shooting of black looters by a white homeowner, Burke makes clear who he believes responsible for the disastrous flooding in New Orleans.

The levees burst because they were structurally weak and had only a marginal chance of surviving a Category 3 storm, much less one of Category 5 strength. Every state emergency official knew this. The Army Corps of Engineers knew this. The National Hurricane Center in Miami knew this. But apparently the U.S. Congress and the current administration in Washington, DC, did not, since they had dramatically cut funding for repair of the levee system only a few months earlier.[84]

Several other crime novels and works of fiction make reference to Katrina. A more reality-based vision of the storm has been represented on stage in several productions, including those contained in a volume called *Katrina On Stage*.[85] The five plays in this collection, all by different authors, were performed in New Orleans in the years following the storm: *Rising Water*, *The Breach*, *Because They Have Words*, *The Trash Bag Tourist*, and *Katrina: The K Word*. In their introduction, the editors argue that "art served as an antidote to the flow of information provided by the broadcast media," making documenting and bearing witness to the on-the-ground experience of Katrina a primary aim of the plays.[86] The idea of countering or complementing the representations and impressions of broadcast media must be more complicated for theater than, say, graffiti or street art generally, as theater takes a long time to prepare and produce and thus cannot compete in the temporal sense. As with poetry, these plays can best be seen as means to express deeply felt emotions and to keep the experience of the storm alive in the public discussion and in the thoughts of those who may or may not have experienced Katrina firsthand. In fact, the author and director interviews contained in the collection reveal a range of such intentions. Aimee Hays, artistic director of the Southern Rap Theater in New Orleans, which commissioned some of these plays and produced others, writes, "I had to do something about my anger and grief. I make theater, so that's what I did, creating a late-night variety show as an outlet for the constant rage and hate I seemed to feel for the politicians, Washington, the Army Corps of Engineers, and for myself and my actions."[87] Anger is also mentioned as a motivating emotion by several of the authors interviewed. All mentioned the need "to do something" after having seen images on television or having experienced the storm directly. Theater is, as Hays writes, what they did.

Theater presents unique possibilities for the representation of emotion and trauma. It can give voice, documentation, and witness, as well as engage an audience directly through an intimate relationship between spectators and performers. As scholars Suzanne Trauth and Lisa Brenner put it, "Theater's emotional impact stems from the intimate relationship the audience experiences in being addressed by live actors who ask them to grapple with the stories they tell."[88] This kind of interactive intimacy is almost unique to theater, though live musical performance and poetry reading can create a similar sense of emotionally charged communicative interaction. The influence of Brecht's epic theater is obvious in these plays and performances, where simplicity of presentation and contemporary relevancy are guiding principles. This is most apparent in *Katrina: The K Word*, by Trauth and Brenner, which has been staged as readings and full productions on college campuses across the United States and was included in a "festival of plays about Hurricane Katrina in 2008."[89]

The paradigm of this approach to theater for contemporary dramatists is *The Laramie Project*, a play about the brutal murder of Matthew Shepard, a young gay man in Wyoming, in 1998. Members of a New York–based theater company traveled to Laramie to interview and interact with members of the community in order to collect information for a dramatization. The resulting play is performed on a bare stage and based on real testimony. Actors speak directly to the audience, changing their clothes and speech patterns to fit the characters they perform. The plays contained in Trauth and Brenner's collection follow this model, as did another Katrina-related play, *The Hurricane Katrina Comedy Festival*, first performed in New York City in 2010. The title of this play is taken from a suggestion by New Orleans mayor Nagin in 2006 that the first anniversary of Katrina should be marked by a comedy hour.[90]

A production of Samuel Beckett's *Waiting for Godot* was performed in the Lower Ninth Ward in New Orleans a few months after Katrina. It was staged under the direction of the artist Paul Chan,[91] who has edited a "field guide" to this production.[92]

There have been many filmed documentary accounts of Katrina, including the many personal videos uploaded on Internet sites like YouTube. Of those that have been professionally produced, several stand out, including two by the accomplished filmmaker Spike Lee. His first, *When the Levees Broke*, appeared in 2006, just one year after Katrina, and was awarded several prizes, including the Human Rights Film Network Award. A four-hour documentary, it was financed by and aired on Home Box Office (HBO), a cable television network owned by the Time-Warner Corporation, which also owns CNN. It was later released as a packaged set containing three compact discs. These included an "epilogue" and a photo gallery with accompanying music by trumpeter Terence Blanchard, whose relation to Katrina and New Orleans has been previously discussed. Structured in four "acts," the film presents Katrina through carefully edited images and the voices of some of its victims. Included are some responsible officials, including Mayor Nagin and Governor Blanco. Without voice-over commentary, there is no obvious finger-pointing, though in his "director's commentary" accompanying the DVD, Lee makes his position clear enough. He recounts that as he viewed the televised images from a European hotel room—images he says could have come from a poor African country—he became angry and hurt at the slow response of the rescue attempts. This was America, after all. This experience led to a determination to make a documentary about Katrina. This again makes clear the role of the mass media in bringing the storm to the world. In fact, Lee opens his film with images taken from CNN broadcasts, which he says were very helpful in carrying out his project. In an opening sequence, along with howling winds and floodwaters devastating the city, we get to see FEMA director Brown declaring in a CNN interview taped the day before Katrina made landfall that he and his agency were well-prepared and would do everything in their power to help the people of the Gulf states. Knowing what we now know about the criticism Brown and his agency received, this alone reveals something of Lee's point of view.

The images and the stories get even more harrowing once Lee moves on to the lesser-known people of New Orleans. Lee works within the mode of documentary realism, and he does it very well. Many of those interviewed on camera are actual victims who tell of their own experience or those of people they know. The presentations are straightforward and all the more forceful for that. The most powerful sequences, however, are not the after-the-fact interviews, but those where Lee was permitted to film actual occurrences. One such incident is the previously described return of the Blanchards to their destroyed family home. Another, which Lee calls his most painful, involves the funeral of a young girl drowned in the floodwaters.[93] Some of the interviews are conducted outdoors, with the destroyed city and the big sky and wide-open southern Louisiana landscape as backdrop. Nature is here omnipresent, a warm and inviting friend and, at the same time, a threatening foe. In the final section, made for the DVD version, Lee allows those interviewed—ordinary citizens and a few local officials—to name those they feel are most responsible for their fate. Blame is placed squarely at the feet of the Army Corps of Engineers and their state and federal overseers. The construction of the levee system is exposed as wrongly designed from the beginning, in part because of limited funding and lack of governmental support. This is obliquely confirmed by an officer from the Corps of Engineers as he explains how the new levee system is being constructed.

As for the aesthetic dimension, background music is added in some instances to raise an ironic eyebrow, but primarily to reinforce the somber mood created by the images of devastation. In an opening sequence, a sentimental Louis Armstrong recording is used as background for footage showing piles of rubble in what was once a thriving neighborhood. This recalls other ironic juxtapositions of image and music in film history, such as the merry tune being sung as bombs fall in Stanley Kubrick's *Dr. Strangelove* and other war films. Terence Blanchard is listed as the composer, and he is seen playing the trumpet while walking alone through a neighborhood street where only destroyed property remains. According to Lee's commentary, the music was intended to provide more than soundtrack, which perhaps explains Blanchard's designation as "composer." His original idea had been to base the presentation of Katrina around New Orleans musicians playing in devastated parts of the city, in scenes one would assume to be like Blanchard's. Had he to do it over again, Lee said he would have called the various parts "movements," a musical term, rather than "acts," the theatrical term it now carries. Lee's Katrina is framed within a musical structure, with words and images from people and places providing the content.

Even at four hours long, *When the Levees Broke* remains unfinished because the story of Katrina remains unfinished, as Lee remarks in his commentary. This helps explain Lee's second documentary, *God Willin' and the*

Creek Don't Rise, which aired on the HBO cable network in 2010. The aim is to bring the audience up to date as to the situation in New Orleans five years after Katrina. The theme this time is rebuilding the city rather than the damage done by the storm, and thus the documentary picks up where the final "movement" of *When the Levees Broke* breaks off. The aim of that segment was to represent the resolve of surviving Katrina victims to become activists in the reconstruction of New Orleans. The two documentaries are similar in representational style, a style that Nicholas Lemann has called "HBO house style: no on-camera host, no voice-over, just filmed scenes and people being interviewed."[94] Lee presents the rebuilding of New Orleans as a struggle between two opposing camps: one that would use the opportunity created by Katrina to rebuild the city in a more streamlined, planned manner, and another that would restore as much of the pre-Katrina way of life as possible. As Kristina Ford describes, there were several "plans" being cast around in the months after Katrina.[95] As the documentary unfolds, it seems clear which side Lee believes won: post-Katrina New Orleans will be smaller, more compact, and, if all goes according to plan, whiter.[96] What for some might seem like a purge is for others a cleansing and an opportunity to rethink and design. Lee presents this as a moral issue; those responsible should do the right thing and restore as much of the city as possible to its pre-Katrina form, warts and all. Those in positions of authority, he suggests, bear a responsibility to those displaced, to see that all is done to allow them to return, even if this means reopening housing projects and rebuilding neighborhoods in highly vulnerable and widely dispersed areas. From this perspective, the fact that only 37 percent of those displaced from the Lower Ninth Ward had returned by 2010 is an indication of the lack of interest and effort on the part of authorities to make them welcome. From another perspective, it might be seen as an indication that former residents have found a better life elsewhere.

As Spike Lee is a well-known and highly regarded filmmaker, one would assume that the audience in mind for his documentaries is wider than just regular HBO cable network subscribers, though that is also a wide and varied audience. Lee's first work is claimed to be the "highest rated, most watched documentary HBO has ever produced."[97] The Home Box Office was created in 1972 and is currently considered the prime cable network in the United States. It also broadcasts in 151 countries worldwide. According to figures reported in 2012, HBO's American audience of nearly 1 million subscribers consists mostly of affluent white men and women.[98]

Treme is another HBO presentation concerned with post-Katrina New Orleans. With a title taken from the name of a New Orleans neighborhood,

Treme is the creation of former journalist David Simon and Eric Overmyer, a writer and producer who lives in New Orleans. Simon is well known for his role in another HBO series, *The Wire*, about drug trafficking and politics in Baltimore, where he worked as a crime reporter. That prizewinning series has been the subject of academic papers and conferences and has helped create a new genre called social science fiction—imaginative writing which nevertheless is very true to life. Aspects of this genre appear also in *Treme*. The show employs professional and nonprofessional actors, some of whom are New Orleans personalities who play themselves.

Treme is framed around a diverse set of characters returning to New Orleans in the weeks after the storm and attempting to get on with their lives. Simon describes *Treme* as a show about New Orleans culture: its music, its food, and its neighborhoods set off from tourist areas of the city. Each episode has a musical interlude: a funeral march, a parade, a club performance, or an Indian dance. Food and New Orleans delicacies are on constant display, so much so that one critic, Nicholas Lemann, was moved to write, "*Treme* is tremendously concerned with being authentically New Orleanian . . . Every distinctive pattern of speech . . . every bit of nomenclature . . . every foodstuff, seems to appear somewhere in the ten episodes."[99] This striving for authenticity includes the use of several local musicians and chefs playing themselves, as well as the inclusion of local amateurs in the cast. As far as the reception is concerned, this attention to detail has led to a successful reaction—everyone in New Orleans I asked about *Treme* liked it, and some reported that they cried often while viewing it.

Politics and the allocation of responsibility for the human tragedies presented in post-Katrina New Orleans are less visible in *Treme*. One story line concerns the search for a young African American man who is missing after the storm. His death is the result of police indifference and bureaucracy, but such a situation could have occurred without the storm. One main character commits suicide in part because he cannot come to grips with the forces shaping the city's future, but there are other, less specific factors behind this as well. Unlike Lee's documentaries, *Treme* is made for entertainment, though of the particular kind presented on HBO. The format follows well-established lines; there are central characters whose lives one follows from episode to episode, and there are "big questions" that structure this flow. The politics are hidden in the characterization. A college professor makes YouTube rants about what is happening and who is responsible for the condition of the city. His wife, a public defender, searches through the law enforcement bureaucracy for a missing young black male, only to find him as a victim of institutional racism and impersonal systemic failure. Perfectly good public housing is not reopened to accommodate the return of poor African Americans, echoing a point made most clearly by Spike Lee. But all of these messages are mixed in with lots of good music and food, perhaps a reflection of common perceptions, or misconceptions, of the city itself.

CONCLUSION

Was Katrina beyond representation? Did it break the established codes or genres? To judge by the works I have elaborated in this chapter, the answer must be no. The catastrophe could be molded to fit into well-established modes of representation. But did these tell the whole story, or can the whole story ever be told? Katrina produced what has been called an unfinished agenda. It is a story that is not complete and perhaps can never be complete, one that requires continuous telling and retelling, with more sides and dimensions, new layers added on and older ones modified. This is a trauma that will always be there, that will remain unfinished and unresolved. It will be part of living memory: for those individuals who lived through it, for the neighborhoods of the city, for the city itself, for the region, and for the nation. Residents today divide their lives into the time before Katrina and after, and the same might well be true for the nation. No one ever wants to experience another storm like it, and we must hope that the country has learned from this experience, has fixed the levees, has bettered its preparedness.

4

TELEVISION COVERAGE

"The media has provided us with a window through which we have been able to witness the impact of the terrible storm . . ."

SENATOR MICHAEL ENZI AT THE FIRST CONGRESSIONAL
HEARING ON HURRICANE KATRINA, SEPTEMBER 8, 2005

"This is not Somalia. This is not Iraq. This is home."

MARK SAVAGE, NBC REPORTER

Intensive television coverage of Katrina began on August 25, 2005, when the storm threatened south Florida. The first reports used satellite imaging, which showed a bright red whirling mass moving slowly around the bottom half of the state. Newscasters and interviewed officials warned residents about the severity of the storm by recalling Hurricane Irene in 1999, which brought up to twenty inches of rain. Katrina, they warned, was expected to do the same. The mode of representation was that of a storm story, complete with footage of wind and water, and talk about previous storms. By dramatizing and anthropomorphizing the weather, one obvious point was to alert residents to the storm's potential danger. The audience in need of such information was real, but limited, as most viewers were not in the actual path of the storm and had no real need of such practical information. For them, storm stories can be a form of entertainment, a source of vicarious engagement: the titillation that comes from viewing danger from a safe distance or the pathos and pity one feels for victims one does not know.[1]

In the United States, producing a televised storm story engages the visual and auditory potentialities of the medium along with the commercial and ideological interests of an industry obsessed with capturing an audience. There are variations, of course, when one compares local and national stations and network newscasts with cable coverage. The similarities, however, outweigh the differences with regard to the mode of presentation. The weather must be made into something more than ordinary; storms must be extraordinary, ominous beyond control, full of character. For hurricanes, the use of personal names helps, as it makes a natural phenomenon appear almost human in its destructive willfulness. Each storm is then different, yet familiar; one recalls the names and what they have done. The broadcast images and sounds trigger this recall, which is then reinforced through the spoken word.

As in the print media, storm stories on television are scripted narratives that include references to previous events—to history, memory, and experience—now filtered through sound and image. Reporters stand tightly wrapped in rain gear, shouting into microphones to be heard above the wailing winds, while in the background one sees deserted streets, bent and broken trees, and scattered debris. Such images are sometimes enhanced by footage provided by amateur "storm-chasers" who take great risks to capture threatening weather images through cloudy windshields and thumping wipers, all of which strengthens the "you-are-there" illusion for viewers. Storm stories are intended to "give perspective" to the viewer by placing the current storm in relation to others they might remember or have heard about, adding to the comparisons supplied by the Saffir-Simpson scale for measuring the severity of hurricanes, which have by now become very familiar to everyone with a television set. As it developed and moved across the Gulf, Katrina was most often compared to Camille and Andrew, hurricanes with similar wind strength. There were some demographic problems of which reporters were aware: not everyone was old enough to remember a bad hurricane, at least not in New Orleans. One CNN reporter made reference to the issue of age and what he called "institutional memory" when he said that many young people in the city had no experience to draw from; they only remembered false alarms and thus "just don't know what it's like."

In appealing to memory, comparisons are important, but so is experience. Television images and talking heads are not enough by themselves, especially for those raised on action and disaster movies. Storms might look exciting rather than dangerous, though of course the two can be intertwined. One aim of such comparisons, then, is to get those in the storm's path to realize how dangerous it is and to make them think twice about riding it out. Here comparisons with familiar storms are important. Besides previous storms, another disaster was frequently cited: 9/11. In one early storm story broadcast, Walter Maestri, director of emergency management for New Orleans, told a CNN interviewer that a direct hit on the city would kill many more people than had died as a result of 9/11. This comparison was meant to have impact, to make people realize just how dangerous the approaching storm was. There are thus several sides to media-transmitted storm stories—to inform, entertain, and capture the audience. In the commercially driven media industry, where holding an audience is essential, a dramatic combination of word, sound, and image is employed for that purpose. Colorful graphics and powerful footage from previous storms help make this happen.

After Katrina's eye (another humanizing aspect) made landfall in southern Louisiana in the early morning on Monday, August 29, a shift in the narrative focus was apparent. Later that evening, NBC broadcast a "Special Edition" of its *Nightly News* show with Brian Williams reporting from New Orleans. Standing in front of the Superdome in jeans and open-collar shirt instead of the usual studio suit and tie, Williams reported that the "human misery is just getting under way." After quickly summarizing the path of the storm and the damage caused, he reported that a last-minute "small tug to the right" had spared New Orleans the worst before the storm moved further inland. The weather in the background appeared calm as Williams spoke to the camera. Martin Savage, another on-the-scene reporter, was called upon to say, "The real story of Katrina has only just begun." The evening's reportage focused equally on the Mississippi coast and New Orleans. The storm was said to have come ashore as a Category 4 hurricane, with wind rather than water dealing the harshest blow. During this report, background footage showed New Orleans police patrolling the French Quarter "to prevent looting," and Williams reported that he spent the day with about nine thousand people at the Superdome. The flooding of the city had not yet begun in earnest, yet the theme of post-storm damage, danger, and rescue—a human-interest story—was taking form.

The following day, August 30, Brian Williams returned to the air for the NBC evening news, standing in front of the Superdome in what appeared to be the same blue shirt, now a little soiled. The opening was full of fanfare: KATRINA in bright blue letters rolled across the screen with loud, computer-generated music in the background. The hurricane was now framed as a human-interest story with devastated lives, wrecked homes, and human misery foregrounded. Scenes of looting were also highlighted, reflecting what was deemed a breakdown of social order, which Williams described as leading to "some of the worst living conditions on the planet, at least in the United States." Though centered on New Orleans, NBC had reporters scattered around the region, and each was given a chance to speak, with accompanying video footage of devastation. Mississippi was afforded significant coverage, with the situation there described as "our tsunami," a comparison to the tidal wave that had struck Thailand the previous year, killing more than two hundred thousand people. Dramatic helicopter-based aerial videos showed the extent of the damage. Barges and off-shore casinos had washed ashore, scattering among the remnants of beachfront homes and businesses in Gulfport, Biloxi, and other towns along the Mississippi Gulf coast.

Back in New Orleans, Williams and colleagues reported a city "ripe for lawlessness" as water, food, and other necessities became scarce. Scenes of chaos and looting, with tourists and residents standing by watching, were shown. Armed with semi-automatic weapons, New Orleans police patrolled the streets. The great majority of local residents represented in these images were black. Interviews with rescuers, mostly white and many from out of town, were also shown. This soon became consciously noted and began to affect the way the news was presented.

Against a background of aerial photographs, CNN reporters spoke on the telephone with Mayor Ray Nagin from his New Orleans hotel headquarters on August 30. At approximately 8:30 in the evening in New Orleans, two days after landfall, the floodwaters from the recently discovered levee breaches were steadily filling the city. A calm and confident-sounding Nagin told the reporters that the city was safe and sound, that there were enough police and National Guard personnel available to keep order. In response to a question, Nagin reported that about twelve thousand to fourteen thousand people were being housed in the Superdome. Their "basic needs" were being cared for, he said; food and water were being provided, though "they might well be stuck there for another week." Plans were in place for their removal, however, he confidently stated. Anyone hearing this could have been forgiven for thinking that all was under control, with the mayor in command of the situation. Images suggesting otherwise, however, were flashing in the background as he spoke.

CHAOS AND CRISIS

By September 1, another shift in tone and focus could be heard, as a sense of crisis and desperation was transmitted across the airwaves. Brian Williams opened his nightly newscast with the statement that he would be reporting from Metairie, outside New Orleans, for reasons of safety: "People are doing what people will do when they feel their lives and those of their families are in danger." A bold title, "Chaos and Crisis," appeared on the screen; after the usual musical fanfare, Williams cautioned the audience about what was to come: "the most dramatic pictures yet." This seemed more enticement than warning. Williams began his remarks by saying, "People are dying in New Orleans today and the city is descending into chaos tonight." He asked viewers to remember that "these are refugees" caught in a "profound humanitarian crisis." Images and interviews, shown in short recorded and edited clips, depicted desperate people begging for help. Reporter Mark Savage summed up his segment by saying, "This is not Somalia. This is not Iraq. This is home."

The aim of the broadcast appeared to be to arouse public concern as well as shape public opinion. The intention was to inform Americans of the plight of their fellow citizens, to mobilize them into action—either by donating money, contacting their political representatives, or simply choosing, as one person interviewed said, "to get off their butts and help." "How come," the same woman asked an interviewer, "there's not a convoy of citizens driving here and saying, 'come get in my car and I'll drive you home?'"[2] Another interviewer asked, "Do you believe this is happening in America, today?" Present in such representation was a humanitarian interest in personalizing not only the storm but also its victims, in order to evoke empathetic understanding. Obviously desperate people were shown; survivors, "refugees," were interviewed, with some offered direct assistance. In a recorded segment from the Mississippi coast, a woman told a reporter that she had just moved to the region and that her family in another part of the country had no way of knowing if she was alive. The reporter offered his satellite phone so a call could be placed, and the ensuing emotional conversation was duly recorded and broadcast.

Like their network counterparts, CNN also offered a "Katrina Special Edition" as part of its September 1, 2005, evening news coverage, with reporter Anderson Cooper as host. The program opened with "shocking images from New Orleans" and Cooper's declaration, "What is happening there is an outrage." This was followed by a video clip showing devastation and desperation, and then the voice-over saying, "This is America? Chaos, anger, a desperate city feeling abandoned." As this was being said, scenes of children crying out "We want help! We want help!" were shown.[3] An interview exchange between Cooper and Louisiana senator Mary Landrieu shown during this broadcast revealed some of the power of on-the-scene television. This interview would later receive much notice and be discussed in Cooper's memoirs,[4] as well as those of New Orleans mayor Ray Nagin.[5] In a split-screen mode, Cooper was shown standing on a New Orleans street and Landrieu in a similar location in Baton Rouge. Interested in locating responsibility for the failed rescue efforts, Cooper asked Landrieu if the federal government bore prime responsibility. He then asked if she believed government officials should apologize to the people of the affected region and the nation at large. In reply, Landrieu began by addressing politicians, beginning with former presidents Bush and Clinton to the sitting president. She said she wanted to "thank all politicians." A clearly agitated Cooper broke in to say there were dead bodies on the street, that people would get "very upset at hearing politicians thanking one another." He recounted seeing the body of a dead woman being eaten by rats after lying on the street for four days. "Do you get the anger that is out here?" he asked provocatively. The senator, whose controlled, impassive face had been shown all through Cooper's emotional remarks, replied, "Anderson, I have the anger inside of me. Most of the homes in my family have been destroyed. Our homes have been destroyed. I understand what you're saying, and I know all of those details." As she spoke, an image of a dead body lying on a New Orleans street was shown as background. Cooper broke in again to ask, "Who are you angry at?" "I'm not angry at anyone, I'm just expressing that it is so important for everyone in this nation to pull together . . . I have every confidence that this country is as great and as strong as we can be to do that. And that effort is under way," Landrieu replied. Cooper responded by saying that people were shamed by what was happening "in this country right now"; that no one seemed to be taking responsibility or taking charge. Landrieu replied, "Trust me, I know what the people are suffering. The governor knows. The president knows. The military officials know. And they're trying to do the very best they can . . ."[6]

From a New York studio, CNN's Aaron Brown hosted another "Katrina: State of Emergency" special program the evening of September 1. Brown began by rhetorically asking of New Orleans, "Is this an American city?" He then described New Orleans as being in a "state of anarchy." Backed by images of extreme desperation and misery outside the Convention Center, Brown reported snipers firing at rescue workers and dead bodies in the streets. In a telephone report, Chris Lawrence told Brown and the viewing audience that he was on the rooftop of a New Orleans police station because police had told him the streets were unsafe. Gangs of young men, he reported, were roving the city shooting randomly and attempting to rape young women. A segment featuring another CNN reporter, David Mattingly, showed desperately ill people being evacuated to a field hospital outside the city. Brown asked Mattingly, "Did you ever think you would stand on the soil of the United States of America and see the scenes you've been witnessing this week?" Mattingly replied, "I try not to think about those things here. This is certainly not the America that I've grown up in."[7] Perhaps with ironic intent, a video clip of President Bush stating, "We view this storm as a temporary disruption that is being addressed by the government and the private sector," was shown in the background.

CNN's evening coverage of September 1 was primarily concerned with looting, lawlessness, and the difficulties police and other authorities had in keeping order so that rescue operations could be carried out. There were repeated remarks about sniper fire hindering such attempts and video footage of young black men carrying various items, including mattresses and piles of clothing, that had been taken from stores. While such images were being shown, a voice-over telephone interview with a Louisiana state trooper confirmed these difficulties; Brown again described the situation in New Orleans as a "state of anarchy." He said that while a promised contingent of thirty thousand National Guard troops had not yet arrived, a smaller group from Arkansas was on the scene and had received "shoot to kill" orders. This report was followed by a statement from Governor Blanco that these troops, newly returned from Iraq, knew how to shoot and kill. The report of armed gangs roving the city was repeated to confirm that need. The drama of desperation and violence was the defining theme of this representation of New Orleans. Brown's sonorous studio voice categorizing a situation from afar contrasted sharply with the visuals and the voices of on-the-scene reporters. Through its power to name, select, and represent, television was adding its weight to the need for and justification of military intervention.

One taped segment that broke from this norm was an emotional interview with a group of five hundred white tourists who had paid a good deal of money to hire buses to take them out of New Orleans, only to be stopped on a highway bridge by the military and armed police officers. They were turned back after being threatened with gunshots fired in the air. One of these tourists recounted how their lives had been saved by a young man who helped them find shelter in a nearby school gymnasium. The camera then turned to this man, a young black male dressed in military camouflage clothing, making him look very much like the looters who were shown in other film segments. In a heavy Louisiana accent he said, "I volunteered to help these people. I've seen beaucoup military but if I can move around they [the people in need of rescue] can move around."[8]

Images of the American flag appeared in many of the sequences put together by CNN reporters and producers. The flag was often shown in the midst of great misery and destruction, possibly as a symbol of resilience, but it was also shown in the hands of individuals in dire need, as if to say, "This is America; can you believe it?" In a dramatic sequence broadcast on CNN on September 7, camera crews followed heavily armed police enforcing the newly issued mandatory evacuation order as they encountered a woman standing outside her home and brandishing an American flag. She stamped her feet and shouted at the police and the camera, "This is our city and we are not going to leave." Forcefully persuaded to evacuate, she was later shown sobbing as she climbed into an awaiting truck.[9] Earlier in that same broadcast, Aaron Brown presented a segment on the flooded geography of southern Louisiana. The segment, titled "Eye of the Storm," featured images of armed soldiers looking for survivors in the flooded river delta region of the state. The pictures, which the reporter called "surreal," looked shockingly like "search and recover" missions in a war zone. Besides fully armed military personnel, there were vehicles resting on damaged building structures and glimpses of lost and dazed livestock. One image showed an American flag hanging in front of a flooded Veterans of Foreign Wars meeting hall. The flag was ceremoniously removed and later returned to its owner in a staged military ritual, which CNN dutifully recorded. "It must feel good to get those flags back," the reporter said. "It does," was the emotionally charged response. This was America after all. The military had brought the flag, and the land, back to its rightful owner.[10]

Other images of the American flag in various conditions and settings appeared throughout the week's television broadcasts. One of the most poignant came during NBC's evening news reportage on September 11, 2005, which had been highlighted as the fourth anniversary of that other September 11. Host John Seigenthaler introduced archival images of a darkened downtown New Orleans from earlier in the week before power was restored. One of the very few buildings with power, he reported, was the headquarters of the local telephone company, where workers raised a large American flag bathed in spotlights against the black city skyline. "It has been shining every night since," said Seigenthaler. "Reminding us of another scene from four years ago today. Another tragedy when the flag inspired a wounded nation. A symbol of courage, unity, and hope." As he said these words, an image of New York City firefighters raising a flag amidst the rubble of the Twin Towers was shown. This image looked very similar to another American icon, the flag raising by U.S. soldiers on Iwo Jima during World War Two, probably the most iconic image of Americans to come out of that war. This is the meaning of the American flag as related to Katrina that NBC apparently wanted to promote, but many other possible interpretations have emerged—such as the flag as a symbol of distress and protest.

NBC's *Today Show* reported in the early morning of September 2 that President Bush would visit the Gulf region. Cameras shifted to the White House lawn as the president approached the microphone, accompanied by Michael Chertoff, the secretary of Homeland Security. A voice-over reminded viewers that Bush was under fire for the perceived failures in the federal relief effort and that the images of despair and desperation broadcast to the nation the previous evening had roused public concern. During his brief remarks, the president acknowledged that relief efforts had been "unacceptable." Called upon to comment on this, MSNBC program host Chris Matthews remarked that Bush had just given the world tomorrow's news headline, namely, "Katrina Relief Efforts 'Unacceptable' Says President Bush." Matthews then said that Katrina and its televised representation had exposed great "fissures" and vulnerabilities to an international audience. One was the "fault line of race," and the second was the nation's unpreparedness in the face of a potential terrorist attack. Both, Matthews suggested, concern civil defense and thus could be rightly compared. The governmental response to Katrina had shown the world how unprepared the nation was. "People are going to be fired," he predicted. Katrina was important beyond itself, Matthews suggested, because it "shows the nation the situation."[11] Katrina, and the mass media coverage of it, had revealed the precarious state of the nation to its citizens. The implicit question, then, was what "the nation" would do with this information.

Following a White House press release, *Today Show* hosts announced that President Bush would not land in New Orleans, presumably for security reasons, as the city had been portrayed as unsafe. This prompted a direct report from New Orleans, where a reporter commented that such fear was unwarranted; he reminded the audience that television crews had moved safely throughout the city and that reports of sniper fire and violence may have been exaggerated. Back in the New York studio, one of the show's hosts cautioned the mass media to be more careful in their reporting, perhaps a reference to the previous day's reportage of desperation and violence on rival CNN. Even as the event was being constructed and reported, the mass media turned some of its attention to its own role.

There was a significant difference between reading the reconstructed accounts of central figures like Ray Nagin and George Bush and viewing their mediated performances during these televised newscasts. After the fact, words on a page, which attempt to account for the complexity of action and to justify their actuality, pale next to televised broadcast images. On

September 2, 2005, CNN's Lou Dobbs broadcast the short speech made by President Bush at Louis Armstrong International Airport in New Orleans after plans had been changed again and the president did visit the city after all. The city was still flooding and rescue efforts were in progress. Bush arrived in New Orleans in late afternoon after touring other regions of the Gulf coast. He appeared before hastily arranged microphones on the airport tarmac, dressed informally in an open-necked shirt. Lined up behind the sunburned president was a row of local politicians: Governor Blanco, Mayor Nagin, and Senator Landrieu, as well as FEMA director Michael Brown. Most of them mirrored the informal dress of the president. The exception was Blanco, one of the two women present, who appeared more formally attired in a business suit. The president hugged her after his remarks and patted Landrieu, the other female present, on the shoulder. The men remained untouched as they stood stiffly behind the president. Ray Nagin was dressed in a white T-shirt with the word "Desire" emblazoned across its front. Nagin explained this clothing choice in his memoirs by saying he wanted to display the name of one of his city's most famous streets, a street name immortalized in Tennessee Williams' *A Street Car Named Desire*.[12]

In sweltering heat, Bush began his remarks by thanking all the politicians present, with the striking exception of FEMA director Brown. Earlier in the day in Alabama, he had praised Brown with his now infamous remark: "Brownie, you're doing a heck of a job." Bush would later justify the comment as being based more on empathy for his beleaguered appointee than actual performance.[13] Helicopters on rescue missions could be seen in the background as the president spoke. After thanking those present, Bush said he believed the city of New Orleans would rise again. This was a city, he said, that he used to visit to enjoy himself, "sometimes too much." There was embarrassed laughter at this remark. Even more striking was what followed. The president of the United States asked the viewing audience to please send money: "We hope you will give; right now we need cash." He ended this appeal with the ritual invocation, "May God bless the people of this part of the world and may God continue to bless the United States of America."[14] Commentators later pointed out that the president avoided entering New Orleans proper and did not visit the Superdome, perhaps to be spared face-to-face confrontation with the masses of those suffering directly from the "unacceptable" relief efforts.

What was one to make of this? With bipartisan political leadership symbolically positioned behind him, the leader of one of the world's richest nations appeared before an international television audience to appeal to private citizens to send money to help rescue efforts in a major American city. There was political ideology as well as symbolism at work here. Many Americans, and especially conservative Republicans, have championed private charities and locally based private initiative rather than government-based relief efforts in dealing with social problems, from drug abuse to disaster relief. In his remarks in Mobile, Alabama, and in New Orleans, the president specifically mentioned the Salvation Army and Red Cross in his appeal. The former is a Christian relief organization and reflects the president's promotion of what are called "faith-based" initiatives of charity and social welfare. Bush repeated this appeal in a press conference during a meeting with charitable organizations on September 6. Entering into the debate about what to call the people needing help, Bush said these were not "'refugees' but American citizens."[15] He repeated his call for people to send "cash money" to these organizations. The CNN reporter then noted the president's belief that faith-based organizations "are a key part of addressing social issues" in the United States.

The Red Cross has a long history of relief and rescue, and even though it is a private organization, it has been considered part of the federal response in disasters. The Red Cross would later come under heavy criticism for its bleak efforts in Katrina's aftermath.[16]

A rather ironic twist in the issue of aid in financing the post-Katrina recovery appeared when *NBC Nightly News* featured a segment on its September 10, 2005, broadcast about the $700 million in foreign aid received by the American government from countries around the world. These contributions came even from impoverished nations like Uganda and Zimbabwe. Taped footage showed members of the Mexican navy landing on the shores of Mississippi to help in the rebuilding efforts. This was the first time the Mexican military had entered the United States since 1846, we were told. A Mexican military physician said in an interview that he felt his country had an obligation "to provide the world's superpower with a helping hand."[17]

The president's visit and the local response to it was the centerpiece of the *NBC Nightly News* broadcast that same evening. After the opening fanfare, Brian Williams reported from Baton Rouge, not New Orleans, again for reasons of safety. Dressed in a work shirt and with his face darkened by soot and sun, Williams began by "stating the obvious, that a catastrophic hurricane strike and the government response to it will in the years or decades to come perhaps necessitate a national discussion on race, on oil, politics, class, infrastructure, the environment and more."[18] This was a performative statement. Like many others in the mass media, Williams was a central actor in the very debate process being called upon. His statement was intended to initiate this debate at the same time that he was intervening in it. This was a central aspect of the media's understanding of its role.

Williams then turned his attention to President Bush's New Orleans visit of a few hours earlier, reporting that a major local radio station had refused to broadcast the president's remarks because "nothing he could say could help save people's lives on the streets of New Orleans—where people were still dying during his visit." Tens of thousands were reported to be still trapped by the floodwaters, stirring "great and growing anger."[19] As these words were spoken, taped images were shown of rescue efforts and lines of desperate people on streets filled with water and debris. It was reported that ten people had died while waiting for help on a dry stretch of interstate roadway. This was followed by excerpts from Mayor Nagin's radio rant the previous evening, with his angry expletives bleeped out. The announcer stated that people felt abandoned. "All of them asking," said the reporter, "How can this happen in America?"[20] One hospital worker interviewed added, "We feel abandoned by the government," personalizing the desperation and locating those responsible.

The following segments carried the announced themes "Looking for the rescuers" and "Who is responsible?" The audience then followed a team of reporters in vans as they drove through city streets and on highways in search of answers. Along the way, they encountered a military officer who is identified as "a three-star general" named Russel Honoré. Honoré would soon become a media-generated hero. When asked why relief efforts had taken so long, the general replied, "This is a disaster, nothing anybody could control. We ain't stuck on stupid!" Other National Guard members were reported to be "nervous," afraid the waiting masses would turn violent. The reporter pointed out that the opposite was actually the case, as people waited patiently under the hot sun for help to arrive. In the midst of this coverage, a fleeting interview was shown with New Orleans police chief Eddie Compass III, who broke down on camera when telling a story about his dog waiting for water and food. Compass then turned his back to the camera and walked away, saying, "It's almost over." There were many interviews shown with crying, desperate people. A reporter said many believed they were being punished by the authorities, as they searched for explanations for the lack of aid.

A segment from Louis Armstrong International Airport, where earlier in the day the president had spoken to the nation, showed what appeared to be hundreds of sick and dying individuals lying on cots in the baggage claim area. They were awaiting evacuation in what the reporter described as a war zone. At one point, the reporter stopped to give a very elderly man some food and drink. There were dead bodies lying covered with sheets nearby. Another news segment then reported on volunteers and support arriving from around the United States. One black woman interviewed in her automobile in Los Angeles said, "This is your family—no matter who they are—where they are; they are your family. Help them." Television here exhibited another of its unique capabilities, instantly linking the nation together and creating a sense of community, albeit an imagined one. It also highlighted a shift in the understanding of the role of television hosts from representing the facts to actively engaging in what was being reported, a change we will return to in the final chapter. This was aided by a Larry King interview with another media celebrity, Jerry Lewis, the actor-turned-telethon master of ceremonies. Before turning the stage over to Aaron Brown for another Katrina program, King and Lewis announced that a CNN special titled "How You Can Help" would be aired the following day.

Brown's Katrina news special the evening of September 2 recounted the day's events, most particularly the visit by President Bush.[21] Brown began by saying that troops and help had finally begun to arrive, five days after the storm. "A week after the terrible storm there is at least the hint that a corner has been turned. But at what cost?" Viewers heard again a short excerpt of Mayor Nagin's angry words and saw images of President Bush walking through devastation in Mississippi, "Doing things presidents do in times like these," Brown said. There was then a turn to New Orleans and its Convention Center, which was identified as reflecting the worst conditions of the post-Katrina aftermath. A telephone interview with "a voice from inside," identified as Allan Gould, provided Gould's commentary that what he had experienced was "a modern genocide,"[22] with "small children being raped and killed, people running around with guns." Brown then reported on the arrival of the National Guard, saying, "When the troops arrived at the Convention Center today the good people inside—not the thugs—cheered." He then spoke live by satellite phone to a reporter seen standing outside the center in pitch-black surroundings, with the only light coming from the spotlight of the camera crew. Brown asked if things had gotten better now that help had arrived; the reporter responded that it would depend on who you asked. The reporter then remarked that coming to the Convention Center was "like walking into a refugee camp in a third world country, the desperation, the smell, the soldiers, the only thing missing is the aid workers."

A report from a New Orleans police station followed. An officer armed with a rifle was interviewed outside the building, which was draped with a large banner proclaiming "Fort Apache," an obvious reference to a popular film, *Fort Apache, The Bronx*, concerning a besieged police station in New York. Brown announced that one-third of the New Orleans police force had fled the city, where, he said, the police were now outmanned and overwhelmed. This was illustrated by a taped interview with an exhausted and distraught officer wearing a bulletproof vest who broke down while speaking. Another officer spoke angrily to the camera as he addressed his colleagues who had abandoned the city. "You are cowards," he said. "When you raised your right hand, you swore to protect this city." This was followed by an eerie video segment headlined "A Night in Hell," filmed again in a pitch-black location as there was no electrical power to the city. Gunshots were heard, first singular and then more sporadic as police answered their fire. The only light came from a wildfire raging in the distance. Early the next morning a female officer was interviewed in the rising sun. She was obviously exhausted and began crying as she said, "This is part two, dealing with the killing, the shooting, the raping." She ended by saying that part three—the recovery and rebuilding—would come: "We will survive, I know that." Back in the studio, Brown was obviously moved by what he had just shown. He returned to the president's visit and the images of Bush walking through the destruction along the Mississippi coast. "How can you show the president anarchy?" he rhetorically asked. "You can show him houses blown over—but the real depth of what has gone on—the real horror of what has gone on in New Orleans—you literally cannot show him. It doesn't mean he doesn't know, but you can't show it to him—not in the flesh."[23] Televised representations would have to do.

The next issue Brown discussed was the role of race and class in rescue and relief efforts. This was first addressed in a segment from Charity Hospital, the largest public hospital in New Orleans and the place where Mayor Nagin was born. On-the-scene interviews with hospital personnel revealed a desperate situation; there was no food, no water, no electricity, and over two hundred patients in need of urgent care. Several resident medical personnel raised what had become a constant theme: "We are in a third world situation." A live interview with CNN medical analyst Sanjay Gupta opened the race and class issue. Gupta reported that while patients in Charity Hospital were in a desperate situation with no aid in sight, directly across the street at Tulane University hospital, a private institution, unessential medical staffs were being evacuated by helicopter. This disparity caused Brown to comment, "There are moments in this story that take your breath away." As he began an interview with Stephanie Tubbs Jones, an African American Democratic congresswoman from Ohio, Brown remarked, "Poor people in this country are getting shafted." Jones concurred. Brown then asked, "How do you think white America will react to these images of black people in giant shelters . . . the stories of looting . . . How do you think white America will process that?" Jones replied, "I'm hoping that most of America, black, brown, white, will say this is a shame—that we are allowing this to happen in the land of the free, home of the brave, the greatest democracy in the world. That we allow this to happen based on race."[24] As the congresswoman spoke, archived images of the desperate crowds at the Convention Center were shown as background. Brown then asked Jones to reflect on how black people would view the situation. She replied, "Black people in America have different life experiences—but I guarantee that each and every one of them, their hearts are going out to them." Drawing on racial memory and empathetic understanding, she continued, "You have to keep in mind that black people in the United States migrated from the South—these people are their relatives. We are offended, we are outraged at America. The democracy is not living up to its calling." Brown asked Jones if the explanation for this sorry state of affairs rested in race or class. "I think it's mostly a matter of class—but clearly race is a factor," Jones replied. Such analysis and blunt commentary was quite extraordinary on American television.

Like their colleagues in the print media, Brown and other television newscasters were intent on opening a public debate on what they saw as foundational issues—race and poverty—with Katrina acting as catalyst. Similarly, NBC newscasters spoke in the name of the American people, a rhetorical expression used by many politicians, when during a September 3 broadcast a commentator said, "The country is demanding to know why [help] took so long to arrive." How does a "country" make demands upon its leaders? In claiming to speak for the nation, the mass media revealed itself as a powerful actor, helping "force the nation to have a conversation it needs."[25]

Television newscasting often involved what we might call debunking. One example was a segment on Aaron Brown's "Katrina: State of Emergency" special of September 2, 2005. After a litany of numbers meant to reveal the extent of the damage caused by the storm and archival images of misery and despair to reinforce the impression, Brown said, "We like to think that natural disasters are random acts of nature. But random implies unpredictability . . . This is a story that was mapped out very precisely years ago." With images of angry survivors flashing in the background, Brown said, "If you only listened to officials you would think it never occurred to anyone." To show this, an interview with General Honoré was presented in which the general said, "No one was clairvoyant enough to see the damage that was caused by this storm." In a forceful rejoinder, Brown remarked, "In fact, emergency service workers and government officials knew or should have known exactly what was going to happen." Brown then turned to the reportage two years earlier in the *New Orleans Times-Picayune* and to one of its authors to recount how they had predicted, step-by-step, what would happen should a major storm strike the city. "It reads like a screen play for what has been unfolding in the previous week," said Brown. "What officials cannot say is that they did not know."[26] Again on September 6, Brown allowed an ironic smile to cross his lips after showing some photographs taken by a woman stuck in the Superdome with her small children and hearing her comments on the horror of the place, saying, "Secretary Chertoff told members of Congress today that things at the Superdome had not been as bad as the media had been reporting."[27] As it turned out, Chertoff was right and Brown's smile was misplaced.

REACTION

By September 4 there was a noticeable shift in the television media's focus to reporting on recovery and repair, the latter in both the physical and reputational sense. The Katrina special reports by *NBC Nightly News* were on the ways "urban warfare" in New Orleans was hindering rescue efforts and the arrival of more armed military personnel to contain it. The city was by now largely evacuated, and images of deserted streets patrolled by military personnel were shown to confirm this. In this new atmosphere, representatives of the Bush administration were shown performing acts of public service, with secretary of state Condoleezza Rice, secretary of defense Donald Rumsfeld, and Chertoff all making appearances in the region. Rumsfeld staked out the administration's position as he emphasized that Katrina was a "natural disaster of historic proportions." Newscasters portrayed the Bush administration as on the defensive and depicted their new visibility as part of an effort to counter images of passivity and mismanagement. The administration was now attempting to use the media, which had been an important vehicle for creating and disseminating that impression, in their efforts to change it. In relation to this public image management, an issue of concern was the number of the deaths caused by the storm and the delayed rescue efforts. A segment of this broadcast contained a report from LSU's Hurricane Center predicting the death count would reach more than ten thousand in the city of New Orleans alone.[28] This figure would prove to be greatly exaggerated.

The power of television was on display once again on September 4. Holding up the front page of the morning's *New Orleans Times-Picayune*, the CNN program host read an excerpt from the paper's editorial, which appeared in bold text on the screen: "We're angry, Mr. President . . . our people deserved rescuing. Many could have been but were not. That's the government's shame." This assertion was followed by a segment about a young Vietnamese American's attempt to locate members of her extended family thought trapped in a still-flooded part of New Orleans. Cameras followed her as she traveled with a reporter by car and boat in the emotional search, which ultimately led to her discovery that her family had been rescued and evacuated. It was a very dramatic piece of reporting. During the same program, another CNN reporter accompanied law enforcement officers as they drove through the city, recounting tales of violence and rescue attempts hindered by sniper fire. This too was dramatic. The by now well-known interview with Jefferson Parish president Aaron Broussard, recorded earlier in the day on NBC's *Meet the Press*, was then replayed. In this interview, Broussard accused the government of murder and began sobbing as he recounted a story about a friend's mother who waited for days for rescuers who never came. CNN reporters called this emotional scene "heartbreaking" and said they had been broadcasting the interview throughout the day. Another segment presented an interview with an exhausted Ray Nagin, who emotionally stated, "This should never happen again. This is the United States of America."[29]

Aaron Broussard's *Meet the Press* interview deserves separate notice with regard to its emotional impact and demonstration of the power of television. The interview took place via satellite phone between Tim Russert in the New York studio and a haggard-looking Broussard in Louisiana on September 4. Broussard appeared on the early morning program, along with Homeland Security secretary Michael Chertoff and Mississippi governor Haley Barbour. The secretary was the first to speak and was asked by Russert to respond to the previous day's headline and editorial in the *New York Daily News*. As Russert showed the secretary, the headline read, "Shame of a Nation," referring to the government's efforts in New Orleans. Russert then read aloud from the paper, "As for Chertoff, if this is the best his department can do, the homeland is not very secure. It is absolutely outrageous."

Television became a vehicle of public service as well as an emotion-bearing carrier of conflict and personal interest stories. On its late-evening Katrina edition on September 4, CNN broadcast images and conversations collected through its "victims and relief" desk.[30] This was a phone and video bank set up by employees of the network to help their own staff members, as well as to help Katrina victims locate missing relatives and friends. Broadcast images included a telephone conversation complete with old photographs as a woman spoke with her father who was still trapped in their family home in New Orleans. The elderly man said he was holding on but had only a few days of supplies left. The daughter then appealed to the nation to help those like her father still trapped in the city. Other segments included the happy face and voice of a woman who had located a relative with the aid of CNN, and of people on the city's streets asking for information about missing relatives. Television here was a tool for connecting victims and also for connecting to an audience with its dramatic imagery and storytelling. Earlier programs on the cable network had told the story of Katrina through the eyes of children, including an eleven-year-old boy who walked a reporter and camera crew through his family's refugee site on the floor of the Convention Center. The appeal to the audience's empathy toward children, especially one as charming as this young African American, was obvious. Such representations were presumably also meant to balance those of slightly older African American men shown engaged in more disagreeable acts, and to complement those of more emotionally distraught individuals. The CNN hosts ended the segment with these words: "Keep watching us. You may just see your family on our air."[31]

This public service role highlighted the issue of the relationship between television broadcasts and audience. Usually thought of as a one-way relationship, as a produced package aimed at a passive and anonymous receiver whose reception is both assumed and conditioned, the effects of television broadcasts during Katrina were different, engaging the audience in a new way. The hoped-for response from the unseen audience was now more ambiguous and nuanced. There remained the idea of eliciting emotions, with the news as a distinctive form of entertainment in a competitive commercial marketplace. This is, after all, a news media business. But added to this was the possibility of empathy and compassion, coming with the broadcasters' direct appeal to the audience to get involved, even if this involved primarily making a monetary donation. The media also offered themselves as a means by which audience members could find and communicate with each other. This shift helped to transform the cool medium of television from bystander to empathetic actor. The transformation brought to the surface the issue of who we are when we watch, when we witness the suffering of others. Are we (as well as the broadcaster) passive consumers, bystanders who absorb and transmit human suffering without intervening? Or are we moral beings, compassionate witnesses who possess the potential for empathetic action? At least some of the reporters and producers engaged in the production and distribution of the "Katrina Story" seemed interested in posing this issue and in altering the normal, everyday understanding of the role of television and its news programs.

During their September 8 broadcast, Aaron Brown and Anderson Cooper justified their intervention and the graphic imagery by saying, "Without us showing the pictures the world might never have known." The reference was to recently discovered, and then broadcast, photographs of dead bodies, some of them mutilated by scavengers, from the Convention Center.[32] Cooper argued that such pictures would help us remember what might have been forgotten once the cleanup operation had washed away all remnants. The claim here is that the media can act as an agent of memory, against forgetting.

This issue came up again in the CNN broadcast on September 12, when a CNN reporter was filmed confronting a soldier who had refused to allow him and a camera crew to enter and film in an area of New Orleans. While the cameras rolled, the reporter told the soldier that CNN had filed a federal lawsuit to prevent FEMA and the military from deciding what could and could not be photographed, and had won favorable ruling. In this case, the issue concerned dead bodies recently uncovered. FEMA had decided, Aaron Brown said in his introductory remarks, to prohibit the filming of the dead and thus to "censor" the free press.[33] The CNN reporter offered his cell phone to the soldier, saying, "Would you like to speak with our lawyer in Atlanta?" Later the reporter told Brown that the Pentagon had now informed the troops on the ground about the court decision and ordered them not to prohibit the working press from entering areas from which they wished to report. The reporter then said to the camera, "We are not out here trying to get gruesome shots of dead bodies. We are simply trying to document all aspects of this story."

BLAME GAME

Katrina was by now a household word associated with distant human suffering. The mass media had helped turn an incident into an emotionally coded symbol, and had acted as a catalyst to stir public debate about its meaning. The groundwork for cultural trauma was laid.

The main focus of the evening of September 6 for both NBC and CNN was what Williams called "the dicey topic of the politics of this," the blame game of "who failed to do what, before and after this catastrophic storm." Williams introduced a segment with the question, "What went wrong?" A parking lot full of empty and unused school buses was shown and some pointed questions were posed: Why weren't the buses used to evacuate citizens from New Orleans? Why wasn't the existing emergency plan followed? Why did government bureaucracy, some of it put in place after 9/11, hinder rather than help the rescue effort? President Bush, under intense criticism according to reporters, promised a complete investigation of "what went right and what went wrong."

The same evening, CNN's Aaron Brown asked why "federal officials just didn't get it."[34] "The blame game is in full swing," a voice-over said. A report on the debate in Congress about the administration's handling of Katrina mentioned that cabinet secretaries, including Michael Chertoff, were strongly questioned and criticized when they appeared before the House of Representatives during the day. One reporter contrasted this reception with that following 9/11, when members of Congress came together to sing "God Bless America" on the Capitol steps. In contrast, on this day Democrat Nancy Pelosi, the House minority leader, had called for Michael Brown's resignation, while the Speaker of the House, Republican Tom DeLay, had blamed local leaders, not the federal government, for what went wrong. DeLay also indicated that things had worked better in Alabama and Mississippi than in Louisiana. A reporter noted that partisan politics had entered the debate, pointing out that the governors of Alabama and Mississippi were Republicans, while local officials in Louisiana were Democrats. It was suggested that whereas the September 11, 2001, attacks had pulled the nation together, the hurricane that swept over the Gulf coast had split it apart, at least as reflected in the political sphere.

The comparison with 9/11 was repeated on September 10 when both NBC and CNN reported on new public opinion polls assessing the president's handling of Katrina relief efforts. Both networks reported that the president's approval rating had sunk to a new low, with 55 percent of respondents saying they disapproved of his performance. CNN added insult to injury by showing an archival picture of the president in New York in 2001 armed with a smile and a bullhorn, arm in arm with a relief worker. "The dynamic is now different," the voice-over said. "This time there is no enemy to rally against. No bull-horn moment." As this was said, a clip of President Bush congratulating FEMA director Brown on doing "a heck of a job" was shown. This clip was followed by CNN political commentator David Gergen proclaiming, "Just as he [Bush] gained from 9/11, he's going to pay a huge political price" for Katrina.[35]

Adding another interpretive layer to the blame game, CNN's Anderson Cooper offered a segment on "local heroes," private citizens who "ignore the bureaucracy" to help rescue people. This segment was followed by an interview conducted by Aaron Brown with three Duke University students who had seen Katrina reportage on television and decided to drive to New Orleans to help. Now back in North Carolina, they recounted how they were able to drive directly to the Convention Center, after deceiving National Guard soldiers at checkpoints with forged press passes. They reported being "shocked" not so much by what they found in the city but by how easy it was to drive in and help the people still stranded there. They claimed to have made several trips back and forth to Baton Rouge with their SUV filled with evacuees. "Why couldn't everyone else get in when we could?" one of them asked. Another said that people were trapped at the Convention Center by "red tape," not simply by the hurricane damage. Interviewed the next evening, Louisiana lieutenant governor Mitch Landrieu made a similar point, but gave more credit to local governmental employees, who he said acted heroically in carrying out their duties as first responders. Pressed to participate in the "blame game," Landrieu declined, saying it was not the time and place for blame. That, he said, would come later—a phrase that came to be repeated often by authorities interviewed on television. Landrieu, brother of Louisiana senator Mary Landrieu, later became mayor of New Orleans and appeared in both of Spike Lee's Katrina documentaries.

Cooper revisited the theme of blame on September 9 when in a taped segment he returned to the now empty New Orleans Convention Center accompanied by a medical doctor who had been in residence during the worst days after the storm. The doctor showed Cooper around, pointing to places where people had lain exhausted and dying. He said he had been the only doctor in the center at a time when it was "hell on earth." Images from the previous week's archives reinforced these words. The doctor said he could still picture the faces of those in dire need of help. He choked up and walked away from the camera, repeating, "It just breaks my heart." With this, Cooper remarked, the doctor placed blame for that horrendous situation on "bureaucratic failure and official mistakes."[36]

Under the heading "Status Alert," CNN returned to this theme over the following days. An opening sequence revealed that Anderson Cooper had been promoted to cohost with Aaron Brown for its "State of Emergency" Katrina coverage. Another broadcast, "Status Alert," was meant to keep the audience abreast of rescue efforts, with daily reports on levels of violence, body counts, and special features hosted by the Louisiana-based Cooper. Back in the studio, the figures presented on the confirmed number of dead were far below the ten thousand first estimated by local officials in New Orleans. This had been reported previously with near disappointment and would be repeated as the reports on the improving recovery efforts continued throughout the week. Thus, on September 12, NBC reported "another gruesome discovery" in New Orleans, as forty bodies were uncovered inside a flooded hospital.[37] On September 9 viewers learned that processing of the dead bodies, now officially listed at 118, had gone slower than expected due to a mix-up between FEMA and the private subcontractor hired to do the work. Identification of the dead and release of the bodies to their families was proceeding much more slowly than in the previous year's tsunami, according to the report. With that in mind, the reporter asked audience members to call in or send an e-mail with any information they had related to the identification of the dead.

KATRINA AND 9/11

Comparisons with 9/11, which had become a powerful symbol of national unity as well as a catch phrase, were repeatedly made during these broadcasts, a point we will return to in the final reflections on cultural trauma. CNN, for example, reported that firefighters from New York City were present in New Orleans to help their beleaguered colleagues and "to repay a debt" for the help and compassion they had received in 2001. A contrast between the two events was drawn when it was pointed out by a New York firefighter that many of his New Orleans colleagues had suffered more personal losses. Firefighters and other public workers, "first responders" in the jargon of the day, had lost property and had family members who were displaced or dead, and they were forced to rescue their own friends and neighbors. Their trauma was thus both individual and collective in a different way from those first responders in New York. Firefighters there had lost colleagues, and their personal trauma was filtered through a framework of professional solidarity.

Returning to the blame game, a following segment showed firefighters from Illinois playing football as they awaited assignment and deployment in New Orleans. The CNN commentary blamed FEMA and its director Michael Brown for this delay. A photomontage with portraits of Brown, Chertoff, President Bush, Ray Nagin, and Governor Blanco asked, "Who is in charge?" The answer proposed by CNN was that FEMA, after a confusing and disastrous nine days, had finally assumed command of rescue operations. In the closing sequence, Michael Brown was shown responding to a reporter's question concerning congressional calls for his resignation. Brown responded: "The president is in charge of that, not me."[38]

"What does Katrina tell us?" was the leading question of CNN's *News*

Hour later in the evening of September 7. The focus was on national preparedness and security. Host Aaron Brown posed the question concretely when he asked, "How safe are we as a country?" The framework for an answer was provided by 9/11, whose "fourth anniversary is upcoming in four days."[39] Reporter Jeff Greenfield invited the audience to "Imagine you are a member of Al-Qaeda watching what happened in New Orleans last week; what would you be thinking?" The September 2001 attacks provided the prism to interpret, as well as judge, the meaning of Hurricane Katrina. Author Stephen Flynn proposed that "Katrina has shown us that we are not better off when it comes to dealing with large-scale attacks."[40] These claims would be repeated again later in the week. As he was speaking, split-screen images showed rescue efforts during Katrina alongside those in New York City on September 11, 2001. This use of imagery aided by technology was powerful, as the pictures made the connection between the two events seem real. This juxtaposition created the impression that the two events were equal in their impact on American society. Building on this, Greenfield went on to draw negative conclusions from the comparison. "While September 11 was literally a bolt from the blue, Katrina was a disaster in plain sight for days, whose consequences were known literally for years," he reported, the implication being that the country should have been better prepared. Such political and policy implications were then made explicitly through a taped interview with Susan Collins, a Republican senator from Maine. Collins asked, "How is it possible that, almost four years to the day after attacks on our country, with billions of dollars spent to improve our preparedness, that a major area of this nation was so ill-prepared to respond to a catastrophe?" Greenfield then concluded the segment by suggesting that the September 11 attacks had shaped governmental thinking about how to respond to a threat to national security. This "terrorism mind-set" had now clouded vision regarding how to respond to "less dramatic" threats like natural disasters: "While 9/11 opened our eyes to the unthinkable, we were blinded to the dangers posed by the familiar."

The comparison with 9/11 was continued later during the same broadcast in a segment on the voluntary contributions to the rescue effort. It was noted that the amount of money collected thus far was twice that collected during 9/11 and three times that collected after the tsunami in 2004. By far the largest amount of money had been donated to the American Red Cross, with over $439 million collected. A few days later, on September 9, CNN offered a "most explosive revelation," namely, that the Red Cross had stayed out of New Orleans where help was most needed, because the downtown area was deemed too dangerous for its relief workers. A Red Cross spokesperson explained that he was told by the local representative of the Department of Homeland Security and the military command in place to stay out of the city.[41] Through this incident, one can observe how television played an active role in the event it helped create. Television aided in the process of soliciting voluntary contributions from its audience. CNN and the networks not only had broadcast images of despair and desperation but also had asked viewers to send money, either directly or by providing air time to those such as President Bush who were making such appeals. Television also provided the means for special programming to reach millions of prospective contributors, such as the Katrina Aid Telethon. And it was through television that selectively powerful images of lawlessness and violence were broadcast into the homes of viewers, including those public and private officials responsible for dispatching voluntary aid. These mediated reports helped create the fears; the Red Cross refused to send the aid workers paid for through those solicited donations.

CNN returned to the blame game, this time under the heading "The Politics of Katrina," on September 7. Aaron Brown opened the broadcast by wondering out loud how interested America was in investigating what had gone wrong and who was responsible. After distinguishing between the politics and the policy of Katrina, Brown noted that investigating such policy questions as "who decided what and why" would take a long time. But the politics of Katrina, the partisan war of words concerning who was to blame, was, he said, already in high gear, with one side playing offense and the other defense, "like it always is in Washington." House minority leader Nancy Pelosi was shown in a video clip blaming the Bush administration, calling for FEMA director Brown's ouster, and saying that President Bush was in "denial" that anything was wrong with the rescue efforts.[42] CNN then showed a video of House majority leader Tom DeLay, a Republican, explaining to the press and the public that the emergency response system "works from the bottom up": "When local officials can't handle the problem, they go to the state, and when they can't handle the problem, they go to the federal government." The CNN reporter added in a voice-over that the local officials happened to be Democrats. CNN's Brown then showed the results of a recently completed public opinion survey, which asked the question "Who is responsible for problems in New Orleans?" The response was revealing: Local Officials 25 percent, Federal Officials 18 percent, Bush 13 percent, No One 38 percent.

On September 9 NBC reported that FEMA director Michael Brown had been relieved of his duties with regard to Katrina but was being kept on as the agency's head. Brian Williams noted that "Brown has become the administration's fall guy for the botched response to Katrina."[43] A taped segment from the afternoon's press conference in Washington, DC, was shown in which Brown stood next to Michael Chertoff as the latter made the announcement. On his other side was the new man in charge, Coast Guard vice admiral Thad Allen. In an ironic tone, the CNN reporter said that while relieving Brown of his duties, Chertoff actually congratulated him on his efforts. Viewers heard Chertoff saying that the grim-faced Brown "has done everything he could to coordinate the federal government's response to this unprecedented challenge. I appreciate his work, as does everybody here." Brown did not speak. The networks reported Brown's resignation as FEMA director three days later on September 12, with NBC's Brian Williams calling Brown Katrina's "first administrative casualty."[44]

In a picture-based retrospective on Brown's short career as FEMA director, NBC used its split-screen technology to refer to what it called "a split-screen America." Its reporter said, "The president was saying that the situation was in hand while television pictures told a horrifying story of death and devastation."[45] Again, the power of television to create an impression was clear. Its power to elicit an emotional response was forcefully revealed in the evening's closing segment. With New Orleans–born Aaron Neville's deep voice intoning Sam Cooke's civil rights song "A Change Is Gonna Come," NBC pieced together pictures and words of despair and devastation, people dying and crying for help, people being rescued and reunited, American flags being waved in distress and resilience. A thoughtful-looking Brian Williams closed with these words: "It's been another tough week and they'll remain in all our thoughts."[46]

CONCLUSION

As in the print media, where cheerful advertisements are juxtaposed with horrifying photographs and fundamental moral and political questions, the commercially driven format of the American mass media determined that the issues of race, class, and poverty brought forth in Katrina's wake were couched between commercial breaks. One particularly emotional CNN program began with a commercial for Mercedes-Benz cars, complete with attractive (and white) actors and a vehicle with the estimated price of $40,525 announced proudly on the screen.[47] While the advent of subscriber-driven cable TV has greatly affected its form and content, American television, including news broadcasting, is driven by commercial forces. Whether through corporate advertising or private subscription, or some combination of both, television stations and the associated networks are first and foremost in the business of turning a profit, making soliciting and capturing an audience a prime concern. The number and interests of advertisers and the number and tastes of viewers are always in the mind of television executives, producers, and broadcasters. The selection and representation of "the news" is a part of this, especially for a twenty-four-hour "news" channel like CNN. The mode of presentation, the attractiveness of the presenters, the technically driven fanfare, the imaging and the music, and of course the carefully packaged topics themselves are ordered and organized with this in mind.

How then was it that both NBC, a mainstream commercial network, and CNN, a cable network, were able to present the story of Hurricane Katrina with such passion and in such a critical way? The similarities in representation and tone are striking. Commercial interests in the mass media have always been tempered by the notion of free speech, outlined and protected by the U.S. Constitution. Added to this is the idea of "the people's right to know" and the journalistic ethic of objective reporting. All these issues came out very clearly in the confrontation between CNN reporters and the resident U.S. government, as represented by FEMA and the military, over photographing dead bodies. As discussed previously, CNN reporters armed with a court order, a cell phone with a lawyer on call, and a whirring camera aggressively confronted armed military personnel. They did this, as the on-the-scene reporter and Anderson Cooper both maintained, in the name of the people and their right to know. They clearly felt as armed as the soldiers they confronted. Finding a way to balance these rights and interests, the financial interests of advertisers, owners, and stockholders, the multifaceted interests of the multilayered audience, and the beliefs and career interests of reporters, producers, and other personnel has been a major determinant of success and failure in the American mass media. Katrina provides an interesting case study in that balancing process. This will be a central theme in the concluding chapter of this book.

It has been said that both Brian Williams and Anderson Cooper had career-turning moments while covering Katrina. The same, of course, could be said for many politicians and administrators, including George Bush, Kathleen Blanco, Ray Nagin, Michael Chernoff, and Michael Brown, whose performances were scrutinized in the media. Both Williams and Cooper found a moral high ground amidst the floodwaters of Katrina; their impassioned styles of reporting, though different in nuance, allowed political and moral issues to come forward in a way that is unusual for mainstream media. This was especially true in their on-the-scene reporting from the affected region, most particularly in New Orleans. Williams' soiled work shirt and apparent compassion for the victims he walked among and Cooper's serious demeanor and direct questions to responsible authorities seemed to articulate (and shape) the concerns of many in the viewing audience. Especially in the later stages of the recovery and rebuilding process, when the immediate danger to victims had largely passed, the ironic demeanor of CNN's Aaron Brown also captured some of the absurdity and pathos that existed amidst the chaos. The exchange between Brown and Cooper described above, when they reflected on the "surreal" events within the reality of Katrina, can serve as an example for many other reported incidents.

The audiences for NBC's early evening news program, broadcast around dinnertime across the country, and the late evening broadcasts of CNN's *News Night* differed substantially, which affected the mode of presentation as well as the content of the news itself. As a nonsubscription national network in a highly competitive market, NBC must remain keenly aware of its diverse but largely anonymous audience. In addition to considering the personality of the "anchor," the main voice and central character in its staging of the news, NBC must carefully package the formatting or mode of presentation so as not to offend what is assumed to be a family-based audience. The evening news is the beginning of prime-time viewing, setting the stage for the rest of the evening's entertainment. The audience is there to be captured for as much of the evening as possible. The news must be informative and compelling, in the best case gluing the viewers to the screen. A powerful storm, with the potential of major damage to life and property over a large area and, most significantly, to a major American city—one with a distinctive personality—provided such an opportunity. Katrina did not disappoint. While swerving at the last moment to miss hitting New Orleans directly, making landfall just below the promised maximum force, it produced a catastrophe in a densely populated area. This was a major story that provided an opportunity for television to show what it could do through its special characteristics, its tools, techniques, and on-screen personalities.

As a twenty-four-hour news network, CNN was in a better position than its regular network competitors like NBC, who were more constrained by the daily news cycle and other programming. For NBC, news reporting was dependent on timing and deadlines in putting together its dinnertime presentation. The "news" had to be interesting, and, to an extent, entertaining. CNN experienced such constraints to a lesser degree; their problem was filling out twenty-four hours with minimal repetition. With so much happening in the wake of the storm, this did not prove much of an issue. There was enough material there, especially when composed in a meaningful way around themes that could be followed through the days and weeks, to keep an audience in front of their television sets for hours on end. This was not necessarily "entertainment" in the usual sense of the word. But the creation of narratives and other framing devices created a need to know, to be informed and kept abreast of what was happening, in a much wider and larger audience than would normally be the case.

What was being broadcast—the despair and desperation of human beings and fellow citizens—required much sensitivity, something more than the usual grim mask and feigned compassion of the normal disaster story. This was personal trauma that had a more compelling force; those affected were members of the same collectivity, a fact that became an issue and had to be argued for. Here race and class became central categories of representation along with the designations "refugee" and "evacuee." Who were these suffering and exposed people? How did they come to be in that desperate situation? Did they belong to "us"? What responsibility did viewers have toward them? Should they get involved, how could they help? These were the issues that guided media representations, largely invisibly.

These were central concerns for reporters, broadcasters, and producers. Put more academically, the question becomes: how can, and should, the trauma of others be staged? What responsibility do we have to these people who we call victims? This was a question for the presenters as well as for those watching.

CONCLUSION

Dear Lawd, Dear Lawd,
De water's comin.
In dis bowl we sit.
Too late for runnin.

BRAD BECHLER, 2009

This book has two aims. The first is to describe and analyze how Hurricane Katrina, which devastated the Gulf coast of the United States in 2005, was represented and interpreted in several spheres of public discourse: the mass media, the arts, and popular culture. The second is to apply and develop the theory of cultural trauma to help interpret the meaning and long-term significance of Hurricane Katrina. In this final chapter I will draw on the accounts presented in previous chapters to further elaborate the theory of cultural trauma. Cultural trauma is a theory of meaning and signification, providing a framework for understanding how and why particular shocking occurrences become catalysts to wide-ranging and deep-going public discourse on collective foundations. To repeat what was said in the opening chapter, cultural traumas are public articulations of collective pain and suffering that require representation through word, sound, and image, as well as interested parties to construct and communicate them. The preceding chapters have recounted those words, sounds, and images as well as the interested parties. It remains now to draw theoretical conclusions that include the ways in which the theory of cultural trauma has been advanced through this study.

WHAT DOES KATRINA MEAN?

There seems to be general agreement that the hurricane called Katrina marks a significant event in recent American history. How significant, and for how long this will remain the case, is something I will address in this closing chapter. To begin a little abstractly, how does an incident of bad weather become an event of national significance? Related to this, how does one gauge the impact and meaning of such an event over time? How, in other words, did Hurricane Katrina become a carrier of great symbolic meaning?

We can begin to answer these questions by first attempting to identify the mechanisms that transform a natural phenomenon into a meaningful event with lasting significance. Meaning is constructed by actors rooted in particular contexts for specific audiences. Turning something as chaotic and unpredictable as a tropical storm into a meaningful event requires first of all a structuring interpretive framework. Besides language and an established vocabulary of terms and concepts, this is provided by narratives filtered through memory and experience. One makes sense of new occurrences through naming and ordering them in relation to what is already known. With regard to a natural phenomenon like a severe storm, naming and coding within an established comparative measure such as the Saffir-Simpson scale is the first step. This helps make sense of the phenomenon and permits an initial gauging of its significance. Naming also helps in selecting and shaping the narrative frame that will be applied. Narrative serves to structure and shape interpretation, prescribing future action through the incorporation of past experience. Calling a weather disturbance a hurricane and coding it attributes meaning and significance. For Americans, Katrina became a meaningful storm when it was named, coded, and mapped by the National Weather Service.

The transformation of this storm into an event intensified with the early media coverage that followed its naming and coding. As discussed throughout, Hurricane Katrina gained in symbolic significance as it moved through the Gulf of Mexico and headed for a second landfall in the vicinity of New Orleans. Not only did Katrina gain in physical force, but it also acquired meaning as it barreled toward the mouth of the Mississippi River and the Gulf coast. The Saffir-Simpson scale was one gauge of Katrina's significance. The number alone attracted the intensive media coverage that helped capture the attention of a national audience. The fact that the storm was headed toward a major American city and a region with gas refineries that were significant to the nation's economy added to this interest. People, including responsible authorities at all levels of office, began to take notice.

New Orleans is not merely a densely populated city; it is a city with a personality, a tourist attraction with a worldwide reputation for good times, food, and music. New Orleans drew attention to itself. This attention intensified as the storm approached. After its coverage of the storm's landfall and region-wide devastation, the national media's attention focused on New Orleans, its tourists, and those sections of the city they frequented. This, it was thought, was the story. Mayor Nagin, who reportedly was worried about the city's image and most especially its local businesses, was called upon to report that the city had "dodged the bullet." Nagin gave the media a confident assessment of the situation as the worst of the storm passed. In the meantime, the devastated small towns along the Gulf coast, particularly in Mississippi, were a prime focus of media attention. As discussed in previous chapters, at this stage national news networks covered the damage and devastation for the entire region, with New Orleans an interesting curiosity. Special attention was afforded the Mississippi coastal towns, some of which were almost entirely destroyed, and cities like Biloxi, where the offshore gambling industry was particularly hard hit. Images of beached casinos and wrecked property dominated the airwaves. Then, seemingly out of nowhere, came the flooding of New Orleans. Authorities appeared caught off guard, surprised as the area's flood defense system failed and water filled nearly 80 percent of the city.

The master media narrative took a turn at this point from natural disaster to human drama: a tale of desperation, death, and despair. Victims, heroes, and villains in an urban social drama replaced the struggle against nature as the centering narrative frame. As this story unfolded and as relief efforts moved haltingly along, the performance of responsible authorities, from state and local officials to the federal government, became a major focus of attention. While victims suffered, those individuals and organizations charged with their welfare floundered. The Federal Emergency Management Agency (FEMA) gained center stage, with its head, Michael Brown, becoming a lead character in what was now an unfolding drama of bureaucratic incompetence alongside desperate suffering. Included in this drama was the apparent disintegration of the social fabric of the city. Disaster became catastrophe. The city's infrastructure began to collapse, with no electricity or running water, ruptured gas mains, and woefully inadequate emergency food, water, and medical supplies for the more than one hundred thousand people stranded in the city. Evacuation buses never arrived at designated locations and the Superdome, the place of last refuge for those

unable to evacuate by their own means, had nowhere near the space or necessary provisions to accommodate those in need. Police services reportedly collapsed as many officers aided their own families or evacuated along
with everyone else. Reports of violence, looting, and other forms of lawlessness circulated wildly and were spread through the mass media. Holed
up in a darkened downtown hotel, the mayor and other local authorities
cried out for help; the city's newspaper called for the cavalry. Though local
bloggers may have claimed otherwise, chaos seemed to have descended
upon New Orleans.[1] State and local officials appeared disoriented and indecisive. The federal government, with other things to worry about, seemed
unsure of how to respond. The president, the person with ultimate responsibility for the safety of the nation, peered through an airplane window,
seemingly distracted and distant. America, identified by many as the most
powerful country on earth, looked paralyzed, unable to accommodate the
obvious needs of its citizens. All this was played out on television for the
world to see. First a regional disaster, Katrina was now an event with global
significance.

IS THIS AMERICA?

It was this social imagery, the emerging sense that the world's richest and
most powerful nation could not care for its citizens in time of need, that led
to the question: "Is this America?" The question is fundamental because it
raises the issue of what it means to be a member of a national collectivity.
What rights and responsibilities does membership entail? What can one
expect from one's country and fellow citizens? The question, first heard on
the streets as victims spoke with reporters and then repeated over and over
again, was not simply meant rhetorically. As the media-fueled public discussion progressed, it was pointedly addressed to the authorities and, more
abstractly, to those witnessing the situation through the mass media.

There are levels and dimensions to this question that can be distin-
guished and analyzed with the help of the previous chapters. At its most
fundamental, "Is this America?" speaks to the relationship between government and those governed. How involved should the government be
in the lives and well-being of its citizens? What rights and responsibilities does this entail? This question reflects upon the basic social contract,
the covenant that grounds the foundational relationship of the American
nation and its people. Is this relationship primarily legal and economic,
grounded in self-interest, or does it also involve the moral responsibility to

care for others without heed to self-interest and cost-benefit calculation? Where does the grounding for such responsibility lie—with private individuals, with organizations and institutions such as family and religious organizations, or with the state? These were issues prominently addressed in the congressional hearings following in the storm's wake in which partisan ideological differences were aired. These were issues raised in the mass media, where reporters added commentary and editorial writers took positions about the failures of those holding responsibility for the common good, from local police to the highest officials of the federal government. President Bush made his own feelings clear when, in addition to promising more and better federal aid, he appealed to faith-based groups, private organizations, and families to lend a helping hand. Ideological differences, falling primarily along party lines, emerged as Democrats and Republicans blamed each other in ways related to short-term political gain and long-term ideological differences.

As the debate progressed, the issue of responsibility was posed in a more restricted way: "What responsibility does government have in national emergencies?" Limiting responsibility to national emergencies made the question less fundamental and systemic. Here again partisan ideologies came into play. Associated with this turn toward the extraordinary was the issue of who should pay for such emergency assistance. Was it the financial responsibility of the federal, state, or local government to pay for emergency relief? From this perspective, the issue was less a question of moral responsibility than a matter of judgment (who decides what an emergency is) and finance (who will pay).

Beyond the role of government in the lives of citizens, "Is this America?" was a comment about what the flooding in New Orleans exposed: the racial and class issues that determined who was left stranded. Televised images from the beleaguered city clearly revealed that those left behind, and by implication those left out of American society, were overwhelmingly black and poor. For social scientists,[2] and of course many others, one could have easily turned the question into a statement: "This is America." The links between race and poverty are well documented. That the majority of those left behind with no means to escape an emergency in a large Southern city would be black and poor would surprise no one with any interest at all in the history of the United States.

Still, the images were shocking: families pulling their belongings on makeshift rafts through flooded city streets, crowds of people stranded in blistering heat on rooftops and highway overpasses, thousands lined up waiting for entry into an ill-equipped Superdome. Most of them were black.

When Georgia congressman John Lewis, an African American veteran of civil rights struggles, posed the question "Is this America?" on the pages of *Newsweek*, he was speaking rhetorically. Of course this is America, this is New Orleans in the state of Louisiana! But did this *look* like America? Did these images depict "the land of the free and the home of the brave" at its finest hour? The implication was that the nation was not living up to its promise, that if indeed this was a country that cared for its citizens and had enormous resources, then what one was viewing was not America. If this *was* America, then there was something fundamentally wrong. Lewis implied that Katrina exposed a systemic flaw which conditioned the human tragedy that was now unfolding before a global audience.

In posing this question, Congressman Lewis and others, like the journalists Arianna Huffington and Jonathan Alter, implied something else as well: that Katrina provided the nation with an opportunity. What was exposed could be addressed—made into a national priority, as Huffington suggested to CNN. Lewis called for a "Marshall-type plan" to rebuild the region, alluding to American investment in post–World War Two Europe. Also writing in *Newsweek*, Alter titled his article "The Other America," drawing clear reference to a book of that title published in 1962 by the American socialist Michael Harrington, as mentioned in an earlier chapter. Written as the civil rights movement was emerging as a powerful voice for racial justice and the impact of postwar economic growth was beginning to trickle down to the American working class, Harrington's book about poverty amidst affluence helped catalyze the social movements and the social policies that would put the issue of inequality on the political agenda. Alter clearly hoped that Katrina would prove the same type of catalyst.

RACE AND CLASS

Nature, it is often said, does not discriminate. In a natural disaster, rich and poor suffer equally. While this might be a popular understanding, disaster experts and victims alike know it to be false. In writing about Hurricane Sandy, Michael Greenberg noted, "Part of the allure [for volunteers] was the equalizing effect of the disaster, the connections between people it provoked where economic and class resentments momentarily seemed to melt away. During the first blinding rush of need it was easy to believe that Nature was the common enemy, not poverty or bankrupt schools or crime."[3] The books by Kroll-Smith and others in this Katrina Shelf series make a similar point, revealing not only that disasters have a way of "mixing" victims of various social strata, but also that recovery, especially in a market-driven economy, reinstates social and economic segregation. When Katrina ripped through the Gulf coast region, commentators were keen to point out that the damage affected all social groups. The flooding of New Orleans challenged this notion. It may have been nature that opened the story, but the human suffering now on stage had deep social and historical roots. An unusual question (for the media, though not in the academic discussion) was then posed: "Who suffers most in natural disasters, and why?" Raising this question required a major shift in news reporting. American mass media favor personal stories and tend toward the personalization of the news. Bringing sociological categories like race and class into the picture added new dimensions. This required conceptualizing the individuals and families favored by the media as general categories. Given the images of the stranded, it was nearly impossible to avoid seeing these victims in categorical terms. Obviously, there were individual stories of suffering and heroism to be told, but it was equally obvious that there was something deeper at work here, that the vast majority of those suffering were clearly members of distinctive racial and economic groups. Once this was acknowledged, it seemed appropriate to address the issue of the social forces that made it the case that the vast majority of those stranded in New Orleans were black and poor. What did *this* say about America? As opposed to a storm story that focuses on the force of nature and the resilience of human beings, where individual stories of survival added character and personality to the forces of nature, the turn to rescue and relief shifted the narrative by adding historical and sociological analysis.

While race and class are usually thought of as neutral categories applied to explain certain outcomes such as who succeeds in America, or, as in the present example, who is most likely to be stranded when disaster strikes, they can also become aspects in normative and ideological explanations as to why this might be the case. Ideologies are ready-made justifications, explaining why things are as they appear and what, if anything, should be done. These too were present in the Katrina debate, though less so in the mainstream mass media. As it became obvious who were the stranded and desperate in New Orleans, the issue became one of responsibility and reaction. The debate that followed was not restricted to academics and experts, but entered the mainstream media, the courts, and the halls of Congress.

A notion circulated through the media during the evacuation of New Orleans was that those who wanted to leave did so and those who remained had stayed of their own free will. This belief has its grounding in the ideological position that the American nation is composed of free individuals, responsible for their own fate. "This is a free country" is an often-stated proposition. Such views help ground another commonly held belief, namely, that if individuals (adults in any case) choose to do things that might be harmful to themselves, such as smoke or drink, they bear responsibility for the consequences. "Please drink responsibly," as the television ads put it. In this view, the responsibility of authorities is, at best, to provide information about the dangers, like the messages on cigarette packages, but ultimate responsibility lies in the hands of the individual to heed the message or not. At its extreme, any restrictions made to protect the common good, such as designated smoking areas, are invasive of individual liberty.

Such views, at least as they are fully reflected upon, find their grounding in John Stuart Mill's famous essay *On Liberty*, in which one can find the following paragraph:

> The only purpose for which power can be rightfully exercised over any member of a civilized community, against his will, is to prevent harm to others. His own good, either physical or mental, is not a sufficient warrant. He cannot rightfully be compelled to do or forbear because it will be better for him to do so, because it will make him happier, because, in the opinion of others, to do so would be wise, or even right.

Beliefs such as these were implied in the mixed messages given by New Orleans mayor Ray Nagin when he hesitated in ordering the evacuation of the city. When Nagin finally did order mandatory evacuation, those who were charged with carrying out these orders, the police and the military, did so in the unspoken understanding that those who refused to leave their homes would not be forced out. This was all duly recorded on camera, as television crews accompanied soldiers moving through the city to enforce the mandatory evacuation order once it had been issued. If those who remained in the city did so of their own free will, then what did it matter which social category they belonged to? They were all free individuals (according to this ideology) exercising their basic rights. What responsibility would authorities and those witnessing the unfolding tragedy through the mass media then have toward them? Was this a national tragedy, a national shame as many headlines proposed, or merely a series of individual tragedies brought about by the victims themselves? If so, the problem could be handled through better planning and more efficient organization, with more aggressive and determined leadership that would not hesitate to act in the name of those deemed incapable of acting for themselves.

At another level of ideology, the race and class of the victims mattered, as their plight could be interpreted and explained in racist terms: what happened to them happened *because* they were members of a race (or class) with particular characteristics and habits of behavior. Such attribution would not necessarily be negative in an essentialist sense, such as supposed inferior intelligence, but could be situationally negative, such as an inbred immobility, clannishness, or hostile attitude toward authority that would serve to clarify why, as a racial or economic group, people would not heed advice to evacuate. Saying "black people" or "poor white trash" are "like that" provides ready-made explanations not only to interpret why people remained in New Orleans as the storm struck, but also to legitimate the claim that one bore no personal responsibility for their fate. Such overt racism was not openly present in the mainstream media, but it circulated on the Internet and could be heard in the conversations of private individuals.

From another ideological perspective, but sharing the idea that race and class matter, those stranded were believed to be left behind and badly treated because they were black and poor. In this perspective, the blame for the situation lies in what is considered systemic or structural discrimination against the stranded. This position was most strongly articulated in the academic debate that followed Katrina, though it could also be found in mass media reporting. American society, it was claimed, has not overcome the racism of its historical past, and this was made evident in the racial segregation of neighborhoods that relegated the black and poor to those areas most likely to flood. It was this fact that made African Americans more vulnerable in the first place. Secondly, when one added class—as conceived in terms of access to economic, social, and political resources—to racial factors, this perspective went a long way toward explaining why the majority of those stranded in New Orleans were poor and African American. They lived in the most unsafe neighborhoods and had fewer of the resources needed to evacuate. Given this systemic perspective, what was to be done? In the short run, the answer was to see to it that those with fewer resources were just as able to return home as those with more resources, and that in planning for future emergencies, their needs would be more carefully considered. Further, the neighborhoods in which they lived should be made less vulnerable and all social services, such as sewer systems, power lines, schools, and public transportation, should be restored. In the long run, given the nature of the identified problem, it would be necessary to combat the systemic forces believed to have caused the problem in the first place. This would mean fundamentally altering national priorities to combat poverty and racism. Just how this would be accomplished was a matter of debate. This debate is still ongoing, though with less publicity than in Katrina's wake. The issues being debated have much to do with American identity as such.

KATRINA AND COLLECTIVE IDENTITY

From my theoretical perspective, what something means is tied up with identity, both individual and collective. Where individual suffering is entwined with collectivities like family, friends, and neighbors, the meaning individuals attribute to a social disaster is intertwined with collective identity. At its most broad and abstract, Katrina helped concretize the "we" implied in the imagined community that is the American nation. The storm and the faltering rescue efforts clearly exposed the needs and neediness of others, challenging those witnessing it to consider their responsibility to help the sufferers. Empathy, like pity, can be a moral judgment in that it can be reserved only for those one finds deserving. Who are these people in need, and who bears responsibility for their condition and their relief? The outpouring of concern and voluntary contributions exemplifies an empathetic identification, one mediated through humanitarianism as well as national identity. As far as the latter is concerned, the question "Is this America?" was again raised: were these victims part of a national collectivity that includes all those who identify themselves as Americans? If so, then what was happening to them could well happen to me.

This linking of individual and collective identity is often neither immediate nor obvious. Such identification sometimes requires reinforcement. In the case of Katrina victims, the commentary that accompanied many of the mass-mediated images of suffering attempted just that. Audiences were constantly reminded that this indeed *was* America and the victims were American citizens. Such emphasis was important especially given the considerations of race and class involved—categorizations that could threaten empathetic identification. The linking of individual and collective identity and the possible distorting categorizations of race and class makes the debate about whether to call the victims "evacuees" or "refugees" more understandable. Given that the majority of victims appeared to be African Americans (at least in New Orleans), and given the minority status of this group in the nation at large, how these individuals were collectively identified became a sensitive and important matter. For some the term "refugee" carried the connotation of a person without a country, not merely a displaced person. This being the case, it was felt that applying the term to those displaced by Katrina meant that they had no country, were not Americans, and thus were not included in the imagined "we, the people."

"Is this America?" also makes reference to the notion that America is different, exceptional, that such things do not happen here. It implies that Americans can do things better, that "we" are a practical, prepared people, with the leadership, foresight, and collective will to prevent tragedies from happening here that happen elsewhere. Katrina delivered a staggering blow to the myth of American exceptionalism, initiating a wide-ranging debate about how to repair this tear in the social fabric and rewrite the foundations of collective identity.

KATRINA AND CULTURAL TRAUMA

Perhaps the only way to discover definitively whether a cultural trauma has in fact taken place is to learn about the minds and spirits of those persons who have been affected by it, and I have not attempted that here. It is an empirical task I am recommending, not one that I have undertaken. I raise these matters to sharpen and focus the question being posed rather than to supply an answer. Did Katrina catalyze cultural trauma in the United States? Did the public discussion that followed the social drama reach into the depths of Americans' collective identity? Were the consequences long-standing and far-reaching enough to impact both collective identity and collective memory? These questions are well worth posing. Katrina did initiate deep-going reflections on the foundations of the American nation; it was cause for public discussion about the nature of American society and the rights and responsibilities of its citizens. There were many negative attributions, and phrases like "national shame" and "national tragedy" filled the headlines and abounded in editorial commentary. All of this might suggest cultural trauma.

Katrina was cause for public reflection on the basic social contract, what I have called the covenant, between a government and those governed. It raised issues of trust and vulnerability, a sense that this could have been me, and if it were me, could I have counted on the authorities to help? In this sense Katrina may indeed have provoked cultural trauma. It clearly contributed to what has been a falling rate of trust in government. However, while Katrina tore the social fabric and reached into the foundations of collective identity, causing public discussion if not debate, it did not evoke a massive political response. In addition, the discussion of foundational issues was primarily limited to articles and editorial comments in the mass media, to academic debates, and to some extent to debate in the halls of Congress. Such debates, however, did not manifest in mass mobilization beyond the outpouring of empathy and charitable engagement, implying that those deeply rooted fissures in the American nation could once again be buried beneath a temporary outpouring of goodwill.

To recall the discussion in the opening chapter of this book, a cultural trauma is understood as a public discourse carried out in a range of forums where the taken-for-granted foundations of collective identity are brought up for critical reflection. In this struggle over meaning there is a contentious contest to define the situation, to name those responsible, and to identify victims and perpetrators. Cultural trauma results from a sense on the part of people that the social fabric of collective identity has been torn and the struggle over meaning just described is part of a process of identification, management, and repair. Although a discursive process, a cultural trauma evokes and incorporates emotional responses; it is "cultural" because it involves meaning and identity, and "trauma" because of the powerful emotions evoked. A more recent example of cultural trauma in the United States is the currently ongoing public debate about violence and gun control following the school shooting in Newtown, Connecticut. This process can occur and be studied at several levels, including the group, the region, and the nation.

CARRIER GROUPS: DEFINING THE SITUATION

In my theoretical understanding, cultural traumas are not things, but processes of defining the meaning of events and attribution contests in which various individuals and groups struggle to define a situation and to manage and control it. Katrina began with a hurricane, an enormous storm that struck a densely populated and vulnerable landscape. Hurricanes are part of the natural rhythm of the Gulf region; there is a hurricane season and a long history of dealing with it. Katrina occurred within this cycle, giving force to the argument that it be understood as a "natural disaster," a force of nature over which human beings had little control. There were also those who proposed a religious interpretation, that Katrina was an "act of God," with some kind of higher meaning attached, as discussed in the opening chapter.[4] As the storm passed and the floodwaters rose, the impact of the disaster spread, giving rise to a new debate about its meaning and cause. Was this merely a continuation of the struggle against nature, or was there something more at stake? The ensuing struggle to place blame and responsibility was part of a larger one to redefine the situation as a social disaster, a result of human error. Here the mass media were an important force in highlighting social and political aspects, thus countering the attempts by those in authority to blame nature and a higher being. The latter were primarily those charged with responsibility for public welfare as they sought to justify their actions. As President Bush put it, "No one could have anticipated that the levees would break," and by implication that catastrophic flooding would occur in New Orleans. As we have seen, this argument was countered by media reportage that argued human failure was responsible for the disaster, from the faulty levee system to the lack of preparation and planning with regard to those left stranded.

This meaning struggle spread into the political arena, to Congress, and to the judicial system, as lawsuits were filed against various public and private agencies. Politicians confronted each other in an attempt to gain advantage or to save face. In every arena, experts were called upon to clarify, justify, or explain what went wrong. These experts were in many instances academics, such as the professors and researchers who often confronted and challenged the professionals employed by various authorities like the Army Corps of Engineers, which was responsible for the flood protection system and other public works. The force-of-nature position was challenged by the idea that long-term human actions were as much responsible for the devastation as the powerful winds and water. The issue of climate change, the warming up of the earth's atmosphere, and the subsequent rising of water levels and temperatures were evoked to explain the power of Katrina. It was argued that the destruction of the wetlands and other natural barriers along the Gulf coast were also responsible for the unprecedented destruction. These had human forces behind them, with nature seen as a manipulated and worked-upon object, not an acting subject or cause of disaster. In all these instances, like those journalists campaigning to enlighten the public about the meaning of Katrina, experts of various kinds acted as carrier groups in the struggle to define the situation and, ultimately, Katrina's meaning.

There were other carrier groups as well. African American intellectuals, religious leaders, and artists of various kinds, shocked by what they saw, attempted through various means to mobilize public opinion and to impact the ongoing debate. For many African Americans, Katrina was yet another in a long history of incidents that brought to light the fragile status of a group with whom they identified. Once again, they argued, African Americans were reminded of their marginal standing despite claims to the contrary in the so-called "post-racial" United States. The furor following the remarks by rapper Kanye West concerning the alleged racism of President Bush highlighted these feelings, as did the performances of Mos Def and Lil Wayne discussed earlier. While such interventions did not immediately provoke mass mobilization, an incident occurred as the debate was ongoing. In December 2006, six black teenagers were accused of beating a white fellow student in Jena, Louisiana, about 220 miles northwest of New Orleans. They were initially charged with attempted murder and conspiracy and threatened with long prison sentences. The trial exposed the long series of racial incidents, including the hanging of a noose from a school-yard tree, which preceded the fight. After an all-white jury convicted the first of the defendants, massive protests broke out across the nation. In September 2007 tens of thousands of protesters arrived in Jena to demonstrate against what was seen as a racially motivated trial and conviction. Research suggests that this protest was organized through social networks formed by African Americans in direct response to the Katrina debate.[5] The mobilization to elect Barack Obama as the first African American president one year later can also be seen as being influenced by the Katrina debate. It may well have provided an opportunity for many Americans to reconfirm any empathetic feelings that emerged during the storm, as well as to express their criticism of the party that had then been in power.

THE POLITICAL CONTEXT AND THE PERFORMANCE OF AUTHORITY

Had Katrina actually occurred in a presidential election year, the reactions of the sitting president and the federal government might well have been different. Had the president been up for reelection, Katrina would have offered a clear opportunity to assert the power of the office and the authority of the person holding it. For those seeking office, playing a forceful role in the debate would have offered an opportunity to "act presidential." As it was, partisan politics played a significant role, as we have already discussed. The fact that the president was a Republican holding particular beliefs about the role of government, especially regarding the federal government in relation to the lives of individual citizens, was an important element in the Katrina debate. Also important was the fact that the state of Louisiana and the city of New Orleans were controlled by Democrats. It was apparent to some that the president responded more readily to the needs and requests of the governors of Mississippi and Alabama.

Beyond partisan politics, the "war on terror" in the United States and the

American war in Iraq were both mentioned in mass media commentary as significant explanatory factors in the Katrina debate. The so-called war on terror set the ideological tone as well as the system of priorities for the newly established Department of Homeland Security. Formed in response to 9/11 and officially constituted in November 2002, the new department was given primary responsibility in all matters of national security from terrorist attacks to natural disasters. As a consequence, the formerly independent FEMA was placed under its jurisdiction. What this actually meant in terms of the chain of command in the handling of disasters was still being worked out when Katrina made landfall. The bureaucratic confusion that ensued in the weeks after the storm has often been attributed at least in part to this reorganization. The competence of the newly appointed FEMA director, Michael Brown, is a related factor, as is that of Michael Chertoff, who was secretary of Homeland Security. At first honored by President Bush for his performance, Brown became Katrina's first administrative victim. The performance of other politicians, most especially Louisiana governor Kathleen Blanco and New Orleans mayor Ray Nagin, came under great media scrutiny. Blanco was represented as a sympathetic yet overwhelmed and indecisive figure. Nagin was often compared, unfavorably, to former New York mayor Rudy Giuliani, whose public performance after the 9/11 attacks was judged as exemplary.

Aside from career outcomes, a central function of the performance of authority during crisis is to manage and contain the situation, to see to it that the crisis does not widen and evolve into cultural trauma. Besides their sworn duty to preserve and protect the common good, those in authority, from first responders to federal officials, must appear to be in control, to know what is happening and what must be done. On these grounds, most of those responsible authorities failed in their response to Katrina. It was not until General Russel Honoré, a "John Wayne dude," as Mayor Nagin called him, dramatically entered the scene that Katrina had its heroic figure. Dressed in combat uniform and arriving by amphibious carrier, Honoré entered New Orleans as if he were leading liberating forces during the Second World War. With cameras whirling, he performed the role of a man in charge, barking orders at his troops, declaring, "We're on a rescue mission, damn it," and assertively outlining a plan of attack. The cavalry had arrived and even the president was impressed. *This* was America!

The war in Iraq was said to have drained available resources from Katrina rescue efforts. Forces from the Louisiana National Guard were deployed in Iraq as Katrina struck. In addition, the cost of the war was offered as part of the reason there were less funds for emergency preparedness projects in the United States and flood control in Louisiana itself.[6] President Bush, who ordered the invasion of Iraq in 2003, was often described as being preoccupied with this war, thus explaining his apparent lack of concern for issues related to Katrina. The same was said about the Department of Homeland Security itself, for whom guarding against terrorist attack was the priority.

NARRATED REPRESENTATION

Many reporters and commentators in the mass media did their best to bring Katrina to the center of America's attention. As with the authorities just mentioned, the disaster had to compete with other "news," but as a story, Katrina had all the ingredients of good copy. There was the drama of man versus nature, the tragic suffering of victims, the heroism of rescuers, and the folly of those in charge. Dramatic imagery abounded. A major American city had been ravaged and a swath of coastline devastated; it looked, many said, like a war zone. With handheld technology and instant messaging, journalists and reporters could do more than bear witness; they could create and influence the course of events. This power was enhanced when the storm destroyed nearly all other means of communication. With its mobile technology and satellite access, the media became a prime source of information and representation, even for the responsible authorities.

Representation is always selective, involving judgment as to what is significant. Incidents and occurrences are selected primarily on the basis of an understanding of what they mean in relation to a story line, what I have been calling a narrative frame. Such frames are preformed, providing already constructed metanarratives that help reporters and audiences make sense of what is occurring before their eyes. Frames capture and shape what is experienced as occurring "out there" in the world. This is a two-sided process, as what is happening "out there" can challenge ready-made frameworks and effectively cause the story line to shift in unexpected directions. This is especially the case when trauma is involved. As I have indicated throughout, Katrina began as a storm story, but soon turned into something else, a social drama composed of set characters. These characters, heroes and villains, victims and perpetrators, were preselected given the story being told and changed accordingly. Drama and personality are two criteria that normally guide selection in the making of mass-mediated news. But as a natural phenomenon and social disaster, Katrina proved so powerful as to rupture the preformed mold. There was more drama and personality than could be contained within ready-made frameworks. Katrina had a humbling effect on journalists as they sought to grasp its meaning. In the process, their understanding of their role expanded. As reporters and commentators struggled to maintain the basic professional norm—a disinterested presenter of a factual reality—some became witnesses and advocates at the same time.

At times role tensions became visible as outright conflict, such as the well-known on-air confrontation between Fox News reporter Shepard Smith and broadcaster/personality Geraldo Rivera with studio host Sean Hannity on September 2, 2005. Hannity opened his program with images of National Guard troops bringing what he said was "hope and order to a lawless town."[7] He then turned to Smith and Rivera on the scene in New Orleans. Rivera, who was standing outside the Convention Center, nearly broke down as he made an impassioned plea for help while holding an infant in his arms. Smith was nearby on a highway overpass. Pointing across the Mississippi River toward the town of Gretna, he said, "Over there, there's hope, over there, there's electricity. Over there, there is food and water. But you cannot go from here to there. The government will not allow you to do it. It's a fact." To which Hannity replied, "All right, Shep. I want to get some perspective here . . ." Smith then broke in forcefully, "That is perspective! That is all the perspective you need." Smith would later explain, "The sheer unbelievability of what was happening didn't immediately sink in with many Americans, including talk show hosts in distant studios. There was a disconnect in the early days of this story . . . sometimes things are just so big and awful that you just can't believe it."[8]

The extent of the devastation and the intensity of the suffering coupled with the increasingly obvious flawed response by the authorities made Katrina difficult to grasp; neither preexisting frameworks nor preformed roles could easily contain it. Smith's "perspective" challenged not only the prevailing ideology of studio host Sean Hannity, known for his conservative views and support of the administration in power, but also those of Hannity and Smith's employer, the News Corporation. Smith would later receive much praise from fellow journalists for his impassioned reportage, while Rivera used the taped images of his own advocacy for Katrina victims to argue against "those in the mainstream media" who criticize Fox News for being politically partisan.[9] This exchange illustrates a potential tension not only between impassioned on-the-scene reporters and more cautious studio-based hosts but within corporate mass media more broadly. The corporate structure of contemporary mass media organizations encourages specialization and such divisions of labor as that between "hosts" and "reporters," along with a concern with pleasing stockholders and, perhaps even more importantly, a carefully conditioned audience. While television news broadcasters may consider themselves journalists with a professional responsibility to be independent, balanced, and "fair-minded," program hosts do not necessarily hold that view of themselves. The same can be said of television audiences, especially those loyal to cable news stations with acknowledged political viewpoints. Such sensibilities must always be respected, given that the ultimate aim is to capture the audience's attention for commercial purposes. Breaking the formula threatens this carefully constructed package of containing just the right amount of titillation that does not threaten deeply rooted beliefs, but rather serves to reinforce them. This is a delicate act of balance that was described in detail in the previous chapter. For some, Katrina upset that balance.

REPRESENTING TRAUMA

How does one represent something that is "just so big and awful that you just can't believe it"? Shepard Smith had a difficult time conveying what he was seeing to studio-based colleagues, but the problem goes much deeper than finding words and overcoming reluctance. The problem of representing a complex phenomenon with a preformed script and a single camera is well-known. This is the case with any major disaster. Katrina was more difficult because it could not be imagined. While Shepard Smith just couldn't believe what he saw, CNN reporter Anderson Cooper and host Aaron Brown (in an exchange discussed earlier) found the situation in New Orleans "surreal," that is, beyond experience. This was America, after all: such things just don't happen here. An occurrence that breaks the boundaries of cognition, that is beyond experience, has become a way of defining trauma in the classic tradition as developed by Freud and, more recently, by followers such as Cathy Caruth.[10] One aim of journalism is to create a story, to make meaningful sense of complex and chaotic occurrences. In a disaster of Katrina's magnitude, this means alternating between helicopter flyovers to gain something of a wider perspective and on-the-ground interviews with residents, rescuers, and experts. What if what is happening is beyond sense, at least as interpreted through readily available frameworks? How does one explain to oneself and to others what is happening? New ways of telling must be invented.

A related issue, that of more concretely representing the trauma of others, concerns finding both a position from which to speak and a tone with which to convey suffering in ways that are not demeaning or exploitative. Something of this emerged in the exchange between CNN reporters and the military as reporters attempted to film dead bodies on the New Orleans streets, discussed in a previous chapter. This too is a classic dilemma, one examined by Dominik LaCapra among others.[11] How does one "offer perspective" when witnessing immense suffering? What kind of voice does one assume; what position does one take? Can one remain the detached observer, presenting all sides and staying indifferent to outcome, the traditional stance and ideological position of American journalism? Or does representing trauma require something else, a specific sensitivity, a taking of sides, becoming engaged?

Similar issues faced artists and photographers as discussed in previous chapters. Such questions only intensify when there is clear empathetic identification. As opposed to artists and photographers composing after the fact and through the lens of aesthetic distance, on-the-scene reporters in New Orleans such as Anderson Cooper, Shepard Smith, and Brian Williams took clear steps in the direction of advocacy. Directly confronted with the trauma of others and the apparent insensitivity of those responsible for their relief, they (and their editors and producers) became actively engaged. This engagement took several forms, from selecting topics and images to pointed exchanges with those in charge. In the process, the medium of television was applied to highlight suffering, to appeal for immediate relief, and even to aid others in their search for information. The cool medium of television turned hot.

This was not necessarily the case for artists and photographers, though many viewed their work as engaged. Their after-the-fact representations were guided by particular aesthetic and commercial interests. Though often depicting disaster with an implicit sense of tragedy and trauma, such works sought to catch the eye and evoke emotion in ways that differed from live television images. First of all, the setting was a different one, as these works were displayed in art spaces, galleries, and museums, which in themselves set the tone for reception. Secondly, since they were viewed through aesthetic and temporal distance, they were, at best, intended to catalyze memory, to keep an occurrence alive and relevant in a world of ever-changing images and incidents. This was clearly the case for New Orleans poet Brad Bechler, who explains that his volume of Katrina poetry *When Will the Sky Fall*, quoted from at the opening of this chapter, was "to get the book out to the mainstream while preserving the memory of the tragedy, victims, survivors, and revelations resulting from this epic storm."[12]

Paradoxically, the coolness of the aesthetic gaze and the compositional care that frames works of visual art can cause the viewer to forget what it is they are seeing. Recall what the resident of the Lower Ninth Ward said to Phil Sandusky as the latter painted a destroyed house. In response to the artist's suggestion that there was something beautiful in destruction, the man angrily declared, "There's nothing beautiful here." The gallery viewing of a destroyed house rendered with all the care and attention that composition and color can bring could easily make one forget that this used to be someone's home. For its former resident, finding that distance and appreciating the artist's "perspective" might be difficult if not impossible. This is also the case with Terrance Osborne's playful rendering of gaily colored houses washed away in the flood; it is difficult to imagine that these were once someone's home.

Televised representations also move in environments defined by aesthetic and commercial interests. They also involve catching and keeping viewers' attention. But the sense of "being there," of directly witnessing the suffering of others with whom one identified, might permit the transcendence of these conditions in a different way than the viewing of gallery-placed art objects. If works of engaged art struggle against aesthetic and temporal distancing, then televised images struggle against overexposure, the viewer fatigue that often accompanies repeated exposure. Even during the first weeks, one could find commentators saying that audiences had "tired" of Katrina.

In the documentaries made by skilled professionals, even the clearly partisan and engaged ones like those of Spike Lee, great care is given to mode and mood. Image and music are carefully selected and coordinated to evoke emotional reaction, as are camera angles and lighting. Such techniques frame the interviews that are selected to provide authenticity as well as deliver a particular message. This differs from the more raw documentaries such as *Trouble the Water* (2008) and *Still Waiting: Life after Katrina* (2007), which may lack the same attention to aesthetic detail but gain emotional power. Like television representations, documentaries make a claim to truth as well as authenticity; these are real people caught up in real events. Yet images and interviews are scripted and selected according to a predetermined narrative frame. The trauma represented is real and staged for the camera at the same time. Take the example given earlier of the powerful scene in Lee's *When the Levees Broke*, when his musical director Terence Blanchard's mother returns to her damaged home for the first time after the flooding. Mrs. Blanchard's shock and tears are spontaneous and real, but the scene itself is staged. Lee "knew" or at least suspected there would be drama here and was well prepared to record it. Had the return not proved to be as dramatic, Lee might not have included it in the final cut.

Such staging places the viewer in an ambiguous position of being both manipulated and moved by what is witnessed.

The audience viewing televised images confronts a similar issue: how to view tragic images while sitting comfortably at home. This general concern becomes accentuated as a moral issue if one identifies with the victims. The fact that this was New Orleans, which perhaps some viewed more as a theme park than a vital urban center, and that the most visible victims were members of distinctive minority groups, made a certain distancing possible. One could pretend that this was not America, not really. Despite all the criticism it received, mass media commentary and debate played a decisive role in fracturing any illusions by repeating that this *was* America and the victims American citizens. How then do bystanders respond when experiencing an empathetic connection, when "better them than me" turns into "it could well have been me"? This is precisely what happened to the letter writer to *Newsweek* upon seeing a stranded infant wrapped in a blanket similar to the one her own child had. Otherness had ceased to matter. Such emotional connection often leads to the desire to help, to act rather than merely witness. Here again the media provided an opportunity. One could offer direct help, like those students interviewed on CNN who drove into New Orleans and offered their vehicle as transportation. The primary means of acting, however, was more in the form of voluntary donations, and the media provided information as to where to send money, food, and clothing.

If the dilemma for the mass media was how to represent trauma, then the challenge for authorities was to prevent obvious personal tragedy and collective trauma from becoming cultural trauma. If such a transformation occurred, it would undermine the very basis of legitimacy on which they stood. Though woefully unprepared and understaffed, many of the local authorities, including first responders and Mayor Nagin and his staff, stayed on the scene and in office during the storm and its immediate aftermath. From his darkened hotel room, Nagin maintained at least a semblance of control until the flooding began. His first public statements as the storm passed were meant to convince others that the situation was under control. The reluctant press conferences of President Bush were meant to do the same. The authorities were performing their role, presenting themselves as in command of an extraordinary natural disaster. The flooding of New Orleans transformed a natural disaster into a social disaster, highlighting the issue of responsibility. As it became increasingly clear that things were not under control, authorities scrambled to place blame, and given the possibility for political gain at stake, the so-called blame game was articulated in partisan terms. Authority appeared at war with itself. This was a process that the now engaged mass media orchestrated. The heroic activities of volunteers and private individuals were contrasted with the confused and incompetent public officials. Until the media-orchestrated arrival of General Honoré, the situation lacked a commanding figure. The only institution that appeared to function was the military, something that might not sit well with the ideals of a democratic society. With the media highlighting the personal trauma of individual victims and the collective trauma of African Americans, negative attributes abounded and foundational issues were articulated.

KATRINA AND COLLECTIVE MEMORY

As this trauma drama unfolded in the mass media and elsewhere, the primary point of reference was not other natural disasters but rather the attacks on U.S. soil on September 11, 2001, most particularly the World Trade Center in New York. For scholars, this provided a measure for distinguishing disaster from catastrophe; for politicians and the mass media, the reference was a means for assessing how far the nation had come in preparedness. As previously discussed, the central difference between disaster and catastrophe lay not so much in the number of victims or the dollar amount of devastation, but rather in the destruction of the basic means of response. The 9/11 attacks killed more people than died as a result of Katrina, at least according to official accounting.[13] But the destruction of New York's Twin Towers, where most of these deaths were recorded, affected only one small part of the city. More importantly, it did not affect the organization and services necessary for effective emergency response. Hurricane Katrina and the flooding of New Orleans destroyed or disarmed everything in its path — flood walls, pumping stations, police services, mass communications systems, and so on. This was the underpinning of catastrophe.

Building in part on this distinction in the political debate, the September 11, 2001, attacks were a starting point for an assessment of emergency management. Members of both political parties in the U.S. Congress and the federal government generally made reference to the attacks on New York and the response there by authorities in their debates evaluating relief and rescue efforts after the hurricane. The foreword to the official report of the Department of Homeland Security issued in 2006 states quite bluntly, "Individual local and State plans, as well as new plans created by the Federal government since the terrorist attacks on September 11, 2001, failed to adequately account for widespread or simultaneous catastrophes."[14] The performance of local politicians, most particularly New Orleans mayor Ray Nagin, was often compared to New York City mayor Rudy Giuliani. Katrina has now replaced 9/11 as a point of reference, at least as far as preparedness is concerned.

As Tropical Storm Isaac moved around the Gulf of Mexico and threatened the city of New Orleans on August 28, 2012, the *New York Times* marked it as the seventh anniversary of Hurricane Katrina.

> All storms have their own personalities, and Isaac promises a very different experience from Katrina. While it could possibly hit New Orleans directly—unlike Katrina, which landed in Mississippi but sent surge waters against the city's faulty levee and flood walls—Isaac will have to contend with a $14.5 billion flood prevention system that has been all but completed by the Army Corps of Engineers. This system, along with its profile and a rapport between parish, state and federal authorities that is far stronger than the dysfunctional relationship that characterized the response effort to Hurricane Katrina . . .[15]

As the *Times* and other media would later report, this time the levees held. "Faulty levee and flood walls," "dysfunctional relationship": these phrases acknowledge who and what was responsible for the tragedy that was Hurricane Katrina. They also reveal the weight of that hurricane on American collective memory. It was not possible to write about the new storm without reference to Katrina.

Then came Sandy. Officially classified as a "post-tropical cyclone" (a "former tropical cyclone carrying heavy rains and high winds"), Hurricane Sandy struck the eastern seaboard on October 29, 2012. Making landfall in New Jersey, it caused flooding and major damage in New York City, also damaging or destroying 305,000 houses in New Jersey and 75,000 buildings and homes in Connecticut.[16] In the mainland United States 132 people died as a result of the storm, and over 8.51 million households in sixteen states and the District of Columbia lost electricity. This *New York Times* article by Andy Newman contained the following side-by-side comparisons: Deaths: Katrina, 1,833; Sandy, more than 200 in 7 countries. Buildings damaged or destroyed: Katrina, 1.2 million housing units; Sandy, 305,000 in New Jersey, 75,000 in Connecticut. Estimated cost: Katrina, $148 billion; Sandy, $71 billion in New York and New Jersey, $360 million in Connecticut.

Katrina became a benchmark for assessing the impact of Hurricane Sandy, as well as a measure of how far responsible officials and relief organizations had progressed since what was now universally recognized as a catastrophic failure in emergency management. FEMA was again involved, and its performance was carefully scrutinized in "post-Katrina" terms. The same was true for the behavior of elected officials, from the governors of New Jersey, New York, and Connecticut to the president of the United States, who, as it happened, was in the midst of a contentious reelection campaign. Natural disasters become measures of social competence, how well individuals and organizations perform in times of crisis and also how prepared and willing individuals are to help others in need. Disasters thus help articulate the contours of a collectivity as well as its organizational readiness. Long after their actual occurrence, Sandy and Katrina were also a measure of the behavior of politicians. Writing in the *New York Times* in January 2013 about statements made by Democrat and Senate majority leader Harry Reid, columnist Frank Bruni wrote, "Noting the Congress had provided help after Hurricane Katrina more quickly than after Sandy, Reid said: 'The people of New Orleans and that area, they were hurt, but nothing in comparison to what happened to the people in New York and New Jersey . . . one million people lost their homes.'" Bruni pointed out the false logic of comparing tragedies based on numbers, especially when they are an invention, like the estimated figure cited by Reid. But that did not stop Bruni from making a numerical comparison of his own: "And if comparisons are to be made, consider this one: as a result of Katrina, 1833 people died—more than nine times as many as died in connection with Sandy. Using the word 'nothing' anywhere in the vicinity of Katrina defies both belief and decency, and Reid was indeed forced to apologize, his efforts to shame his Republican foes having brought a full measure of shame to his own doorstep."

As a category foundational to the American consciousness, race entered the picture almost immediately. New Orleans is a Southern city, one with a long history of racial tension and segregation rooted in slavery. The vast majority of those appearing in media representations were black, and this also made New Orleans and Katrina "different." As a country of immigrants, America lives and trades on difference, as well as on a profound belief in individual freedom. Creating a sense of community, a commonweal, has always been problematic. This is the case from the mythical frontier, where the forging of a law-abiding community was always a central theme in aesthetic representations, to the political and cultural issues involved in integrating the waves of immigrants that flooded American shores. This dilemma is compounded in times of great crisis when the collective will needs to be mobilized on a national level, such as in wartime. Rallying around the flag and forging a sense of common purpose among individuals from various backgrounds and regions of the nation has always been a central theme of war films, where ethnic diversity and stereotyping (the Jewish kid from New York, the black or white southerner, the working-class white from Brooklyn, the farm boy from Iowa or Kansas) have been prominently on display. The mass media, including films and popular culture, have been a very important mechanism in this process, from President Roosevelt's fireside chats during World War Two to the thinly veiled propaganda produced by Hollywood.

Many working in and around the mass media tried to convince the country that Katrina presented a similar crisis, a national crisis requiring mobilization of the national will and creation of a sense of national community in which everyone bears responsibility for the welfare of their fellow citizens. Acknowledging this effort helps explain the type of rhetoric being used. It also helps us understand the sensitivity to the use of such terms as "refugees," to which some black intellectuals objected because, they believed, it suggested that those desperate survivors of New Orleans were not American citizens. This sort of advocacy in the mainstream media is unusual in that it breaks with the unspoken norm of acting as guardians of public order and morale. As Susan Sontag has pointed out, editorial self-censorship comes into play with regard to publishing photographs that might be considered in "bad taste," such as photographs of a nation's dead soldiers which might be detrimental to governmental efforts to promote war.[17] In the case of Katrina, this seems to have been suspended, or at least modified to the extent that there was an interest in some mainstream media in mobilizing public opinion, which altered what was considered to be in good taste.

Saying that the images and stories presented through the mass media were meant to move public opinion in a particular direction does not mean that these efforts were insincere or disingenuous, or even that there necessarily existed a conscious intention to manipulate the public. For those higher up in the organizational hierarchy, it was most certainly a sensitive issue and was most likely discussed. Editorial writers made this effort most consciously and probably had to weigh the sensitivities of their bosses, those who might have felt the eyes of advertisers and stockholders upon them, when choosing what images and story lines to present. It means they saw a real problem and also a way to resolve it. Reporters and newscasters, especially those on the scene, were greatly moved by what they saw. As noted, many of those working for the *Times-Picayune*, for example, suffered great personal loss from the storm (though a cynic could argue they wanted government aid to rebuild and replace their losses), and the reported conflicts between on-the-scene reporters and their networks reflect a sincerity in the desire to report what they saw and experienced, rather than what the advertisers or the corporate heads wanted to hear or have reported. In the reporters' minds was the notion that the crisis they saw could not be resolved locally, that local and regional authorities, whatever their personal competencies, were swamped, overwhelmed by the scale and scope of this disaster. Responding to the disaster would require a large-scale national effort, and this is what they hoped to mobilize. This was most clearly stated in the editorial comments and in the signed commentaries.

FINAL REFLECTIONS

This book will appear in print on the tenth anniversary of Katrina, which means the time has come for us to pursue the query I have focused on: what is the lasting heritage of Katrina on the American consciousness? Did Katrina burst the bounds of our understanding? Did it lay open the ideational foundations of the American nation, making them available for public reflection? Did Katrina evoke cultural trauma, and if so, for whom?

Katina burst or at least tested boundaries in several areas of discourse. The mass media format of covering weather stories was altered significantly, most especially in the realms of narrative framing and on-the-scene reporting. Reporting in print and on television tested the role of the journalist and fractured preformed scripts. Journalists became public intellectuals, emotionally and politically engaged in what they were meant to report. They took stands, named perpetrators, and empathized with victims. They applied sociological categories and analyzed what they were describing from a theoretically informed critical perspective. Of course, this did not apply to all or perhaps even most journalists, and there were many, including local journalists and on-the-scene bloggers, who were outraged by much of the media reporting, especially in the early stages of the storm. But as I hope to have shown, there were significant numbers of journalists who joined the ranks of academics in presenting powerful social criticism in the course of their everyday reporting. In this, they tested and sometimes crossed the boundaries of their professional roles, becoming advocates as well as social critics.

Katrina laid bare cleavages in the American collectivity, that imagined community we call a nation. The flooding of New Orleans put race, poverty, and the treatment of the elderly on display for the entire world to see. The desperate people awaiting care and rescue in long lines outside the Superdome, on rooftops, and on highway overpasses were overwhelmingly African American and poor, many of them women and children. They were left behind because they were left out, having neither the means nor the opportunity to reach safety. A significant number of those who remained in the city did so in order to care for elderly or sickly relatives or neighbors. The first deaths reported by the mass media were those of elderly residents trapped and left to die in a nursing home. What was made visible in words and images through the mass media became a catalyst for political debate in the halls of Congress and was then reflected back through the media to the general public. Foundational issues grounding American collective identity were raised and reflected upon. Negative attributes abounded in headlines and editorial commentary: Katrina was a "National Tragedy" and a "National Shame." This was most profoundly captured in the often-raised question, "Is this America?" In the struggle to define what Katrina meant, perpetrators and victims were named, reasons and causes were sought after, and blame was placed. The issue of how the richest and most powerful nation on earth could leave its citizens suffering for so long resounded in the public debate. The debate went on for months and, especially for the victims and for African Americans generally, is still ongoing.

Katrina has left an indelible mark on American collective memory, not merely as a severe storm but as a social disaster, a catastrophe which revealed the nation at its worst. In this sense, Katrina marks American collective memory in a similar yet different way from 9/11, another infamous event. That attack came from outside. It had clear villains and, with the help of media orchestration, heroes and victims. This helped create a belief that it was the nation that was attacked, and those who identified themselves as members of that collectivity could rally around a sense of violation. Collective identity was not threatened; rather it was strengthened, though an exception must be made for American Muslims.[18] Katrina did none of this. It revealed the flaws and fractions of the nation, and while many were moved to empathetic identification with its victims, the flags that were waved after the storm were seldom waved out of patriotic pride.

While both 9/11 and Katrina can be analyzed through the theory of cultural trauma, they reside in separate compartments of American collective memory. Their meanings are also different, as are the carrier groups that bear it. Like December 7, 1941, the "day of infamy" when the Japanese attacked an American military base at Pearl Harbor, 9/11 will be similarly remembered as an unwarranted violation of national honor by a foreign enemy. It too was used to justify a "war" and the eventual assassination of the main perpetrator, Osama bin Laden. The main carrier groups of its memory, the families of the victims on the one hand and politically motivated individuals and groups on the other, are sometimes at cross-purposes.

However, 9/11 is generally evoked as a means of creating national unity, set against an outside political threat. This allows one to make distinctions between Katrina and 9/11 in comparing their impact as national traumas.

The flood protection system around New Orleans has been vastly improved and awaits the next storm season. In a strange way, these new massive structures have become monuments to Katrina. When one sees them or shows them to others, one is reminded of the storm that called them into being. The new flood walls are unintended memorials to the storm and the flooding that followed. The Army Corps of Engineers has acknowledged and apologized for its failures; FEMA has been refurbished and given a more clearly defined profile and focus. The city of New Orleans has regained its personality and much of its population, though poorer neighborhoods like the symbolic Lower Ninth Ward lag far behind and will probably never be the same again. The same can be said of the American nation.

NOTES

CHAPTER ONE

1. Bellah 1991.

2. An alternative to the idea of a covenant, which has religious connotations, is to describe the relations between a government and its citizens as a social contract. Michael Ignatieff (2005) uses this language to speak of the failures of the response to Katrina. Ignatieff called his powerful condemnation of governmental relief efforts "The Broken Contract." I prefer the term "covenant" to highlight the uniqueness of the American understanding of the relationship between state and citizen, which emphasizes religiosity.

3. Brinkley 2006: 32.

4. *New Orleans Times-Picayune*, September 9, 2005, www.nola.com.

5. Brinkley 2006: 21, 24.

6. Gordon Russell, *Times-Picayune*, August 28, 2005, www.nola.com.

7. Brinkley 2006: 203.

8. Ibid.

9. Quoted in ibid.: 4.

10. http://whatreallyhappened.com/WRHARTICLES/Orleans_levees.html.

11. Erikson 1994: 226 ff.

12. Ibid.: 232.

13. Neal 1998.

14. Steinberg 2000.

15. Brinkley 2006: 618.

16. Olick, 2007.

17. http://geophysics-old.tau.ac.il/personal/shumlik/LisbonEq-letters.htm.

18. Neiman 2005.

19. *New York Times*, January 24, 2010, op-ed.

20. Dyson 2005: 33.

21. www.brookings.edu/opinions/2006/0804cities_katz.aspx?p=1.

22. Ibid.: 2.

23. Dyson 2005: 5.

24. See Dyson 2005: 26 ff for a full account.

25. Cited in Dyson 2005: 20.

26. Eyerman 2011.

CHAPTER TWO

1. Sylvester 2008: 1.
2. McQuaid and Schleifstein 2006: 227. NPR correspondent John Burnett, who watched the storm arrive from his balcony at a Hilton Hotel in downtown New Orleans, explained this "mistake" by saying that "most journalists were staying near the French Quarter, which seemed fine" (quoted in Sylvester 2008: 170).
3. Sylvester 2009: 3.
4. Quoted in McQuaid and Schleifstein 2006: 309.
5. Quoted in ibid.: 299.
6. Ibid.: 240.
7. http://nytimes.com/2005/09/05.business/media/05picayune.htm.
8. Horne 2006: 111.
9. Mark Schleifstein, in correspondence with the author, March 15, 2012.
10. Interview with Mark Schleifstein, February 2, 2012. He also reported that 32 percent of the Army Corps of Engineers staff lost their homes.
11. Interview with Jim Amoss, February 2, 2012.
12. New Orleans had a total population of 1.2 million, of which 100,000 stayed during the storm, according to figures presented at the exhibition at the Louisiana State Museum on Jackson Square, January 2012.
13. Gwen Filosa, *New Orleans Times-Picayune*, August 29, 2005.
14. McQuaid and Schleifstein 2006: 209.
15. This dilemma was the subject of the film *Medium Cool* and a topic of deep concern for those who worked in or studied the mass media, including theorist Marshall McLuhan.
16. McQuaid and Schleifstein 2006: 243.
17. *Times-Picayune*, August 29, 2005, www.nola.com.
18. Swenson 2011: 12.
19. *New York Times*, August 31, 2005, A11.
20. Ibid.: A18.
21. Interview, February 2, 2012.
22. Story by Brian Thevenot, who would write about media reporting after the hurricane.
23. *New York Times*, September 4, 2005, "Week in Review" section 4, p. 1.
24. For a full account, see McQuaid and Schleifstein, reporters for the *Times-Picayune* in 2002 when they wrote an award-winning series of articles on the dangers to the Louisiana coast.
25. *Times-Picayune*, September 2, 2005.
26. McQuaid and Schleifstein 2006: 342.
27. *New York Times*, September 3, 2005.
28. *Newsweek*, September 12, 2005: 88.
29. *New York Times*, September 3, 2005: A20.

30. Smelser in Alexander et al. 2004.

31. *New York Times*, September 4, 2005: 26.

32. Caruth 1996.

33. Dyson, Boyd-Franklin 2010; Sommers et al. 2006.

34. Eyerman 2011.

35. *Newsweek*, September 12, 2005: 53.

36. Ibid.: 52.

37. *Newsweek*, September 26, 2005: 18.

38. Ibid.: 18.

39. *Newsweek*, September 19, 2005: 4.

40. Ibid.

41. Ibid.: 42.

42. Ibid.

43. Ibid.: 44.

44. Ibid.: 45.

45. Ibid.: 42.

46. Ibid.: 48.

47. *Time*, September 12, 2005.

48. Ibid.: 5.

49. Ibid.: 27.

50. Ibid.: 54.

51. Ibid.

52. Ibid.

53. Ibid.: 54.

54. Ibid.

55. Ibid.: 58.

56. *Time*, September 19, 2005: 34–41.

57. Ibid.: 42.

58. *Time*, September 26, 2005.

59. Hall 1980.

CHAPTER THREE

1. *New York Times*, March 1, 2012.

2. Negra 2010: 6.

3. In ibid.

4. Eyerman 2008.

5. Rose 2007: 101.

6. Both quoted in Swenson 2011: 11.

7. Cohn 2007.

8. *New York Times*, August 27, 2010.

9. Swenson 2011: 37 ff.

10. Spera 2011; see Regis and Walton 2008 for a more extensive analysis of the Jazz and Heritage Festival.

11. Swenson 2011.

12. The New Orleans Musicians Hurricane Relief Fund originated from Preservation Hall, a New Orleans club dedicated to preserving and promoting the city's jazz traditions. Tipitina's Foundation is a nonprofit organization founded in 2003. Its stated mission is "[t]o support Louisiana and New Orleans' irreplaceable musical community and preserve their unique musical culture." Tipitina's Uptown, a musical venue located in the Uptown district of the city, was founded as a venue for Professor Longhair's funk in 1977. Other organizations included MusiCares, Sweet Home New Orleans, and the New Orleans Music Clinic. See Swenson 2011: 44.

13. Libra LaGrone quoted in Swenson 2011: 36.

14. Rose 2007.

15. Quoted in Spera 2010: 117–118.

16. Quoted in ibid.: 118–119.

17. Ibid.

18. Ibid.: 120.

19. Swenson 2011: 49.

20. Quoted in ibid.: 49.

21. Ibid.: 160–161.

22. Ibid.: 212.

23. Quoted in Swenson 2011: 213.

24. Ibid.: 214.

25. Ibid.

26. Rebennack 1994: 15.

27. Raeburn (2007) recounts suggestions that this song become Louisiana's new state anthem to replace the more upbeat "You Are My Sunshine." In his insightful article, he makes the point that "New Orleans jazz musicians have an indulged predilection for escapism." They have preferred to emphasize the more hedonistic aspects of human behavior rather than social commentary on floods and other disasters. Thus, "You Are My Sunshine," he suggests, might remain more fitting as the state's anthem, even post-Katrina.

28. YouTube; see also Spera 2011: 67.

29. There is even a ranking of the top five Katrina-related rap songs: 1. Lil Wayne featuring Robin Thicke, "Tie My Hands"; 2. Mos Def, "Dollar Day (Katrina Klap)"; 3. Public Enemy, "Hell No. We Ain't Alright"; 4. The Legendary K. O., "George Bush Don't Like Black People"; 5. OutKast featuring Lil Wayne and Snoop Dogg, "Hollywood Divorce." http://blogs.houstonpress.com/rocks/2010/08/the_top_five _hurricane_katrina.php.

30. In 2007 the *New Yorker* named Lil Wayne "Rapper of the Year."

31. Cohn 2007: 230.

32. www.youtube.com/watch?v=4w_6zGJ6Xts.

33. www.youtube.com/watch?v=nJnBhGaks6oerview.

34. It should also be noted that on the other side of the political spectrum one finds such groups as Dirty White Punks, a neo-Nazi band from Austin, Texas, who released a song called "Thank You Katrina." The "thank you" is for washing away African Americans.

35. Swenson 2011: 68.

36. Sontag 2003.

37. Ibid.: 61.

38. Hall 1980.

39. Regis 2001.

40. Breunlin and Regis 2006.

41. Swenson 2011: 105 ff.

42. Ibid.: 99.

43. Mayer 2008.

44. Ibid.: 179.

45. Sontag 2003: 76.

46. Mayer 2008: 178.

47. Sontag 2003: 76.

48. Mayer 2008: 178.

49. Ibid.: 180.

50. Sandusky 2007: 16.

51. Ibid.: 14.

52. Ibid.

53. Ibid.: 15.

54. Ibid.: 16.

55. Carl Little in Bates 2010: 16.

56. Ibid.: 17–20.

57. Ibid.: 20.

58. Sandusky 2007: 14.

59. Swenson 2011: 178.

60. Fuqua 2010.

61. Interview in ibid.

62. Ibid.

63. Ibid.

64. Napoli video interview, www.floodwall.org/jana_interview.html.

65. Ibid.

66. Fuqua 2010.

67. Ibid.: 55.

68. Ibid.: 50.

69. Ibid.: 50.

70. Ibid.: 51.

71. Trethewey 2010: 56–57.

72. Ibid.: 57.

73. Fuqua 2010.
74. Negra 2010.
75. Ibid.: 1.
76. Trethewey 2010: 58.
77. Bechler 2009.
78. Biguenet et al. 2010.
79. Relle in ibid.: 20.
80. Spielman 2007.
81. Ibid.: 1–2.
82. Ibid.: 2.
83. Burke 2007.
84. Ibid.: 42.
85. Trauth and Brenner 2011.
86. Ibid.: ix.
87. Ibid.: 246.
88. Ibid.: x.
89. Ibid.: 205.
90. *New York Times*, August 17, 2010.
91. Chan 2010.
92. See also Fuqua 2010: 43.
93. http://www.mosaec/television/tv_whentheleveesbroke.htm.
94. Lemann 2011.
95. Ford 2010.
96. Lemann 2011.
97. www.mosaec/television/tv_whentheleveesbroke.htm.
98. http://www.quantcast.com.
99. Lemann 2010: 7.

CHAPTER FOUR

1. Vannini and McCright 2007.
2. NBC, September 1, 2005.
3. http://transcripts.cnn.com.
4. Cooper 2010.
5. Nagin 2010.
6. http://transcripts.cnn.com/TRANSCRIPTS/050901/acd.01.html, also available on *YouTube*.
7. Vanderbilt Television News Archive.
8. Ibid.
9. Ibid.: 1001.
10. Ibid.: 930.
11. Ibid.: 800.

12. Nagin 2010.

13. Bush 2010.

14. Vanderbilt Archive.

15. Ibid.: 1112.

16. Brinkley 2006: 588.

17. Vanderbilt Archive: 542.

18. Ibid.: 531.

19. Ibid.: 531.

20. Ibid.: 531.

21. Ibid.: 900.

22. *CNN Reports* 2005.

23. Ibid.

24. Ibid.: 930.

25. NBC commentator, September 3.

26. Vanderbilt Archive: 1030.

27. Ibid.: 1043.

28. Ibid.: 530.

29. Ibid.: 900.

30. Ibid.: 953.

31. Ibid.: 958.

32. Ibid.: 900.

33. Ibid.: 900.

34. Ibid.: 900.

35. Ibid.: 917.

36. Ibid.: 1015.

37. Ibid.: 530.

38. Ibid.: 921.

39. Ibid.: 1021.

40. Flynn 2005.

41. Vanderbilt Archive: 917.

42. Ibid.: 1018.

43. Ibid.: 530.

44. Ibid.: 530.

45. Ibid.: 530.

46. Ibid.: 556.

47. As broadcast from the local Nashville affiliate.

CONCLUSION

1. On bloggers, see Ostertag and Ortiz 2013.

2. Such as Christopher Jenks, quoted in the opening chapter.

3. Greenberg 2013: 14.

4. See Steinberg 2000.

5. Greenlea 2014.

6. Zunes 2005.

7. http://www.youtube.com/watch?v=OPswpqB73SA.

8. Bauder 2005.

9. http://www.youtube.com/watch?v=YMurpSbPxC8.

10. Caruth 1996.

11. LaCapra 2001.

12. Interviewed on wordpress.com, http://houseonahillorg.blogspot.com/2009 /07/anniversary-of-hurricaneKatrina-is-one.html.

13. 2,981 versus 1,330, Department of Homeland Security 2006: 211.

14. Department of Homeland Security 2006: 1.

15. *New York Times*, August 28, 2012: A16.

16. Ibid., November 27, 2012.

17. Sontag 2003: 68–69.

18. Peek 2010.

BIBLIOGRAPHY

Acharya, Khagendra (2012). "Thinking through Media Theories: Understanding and Furthering Trauma Studies." *Continental Journal Arts and Humanities* 4(2): 8–17.

Alexander, Jeffrey, Ron Eyerman, Bernhard Giesen, Neil Smelser, Piotr Sztompka (eds.) (2004). *Cultural Trauma and Collective Identity*. Berkeley: University of California Press.

"Antonia" (2012). "Estaba Reclamando Mi Sudor" (I Was Demanding What I Earned with My Sweat). In David and Enarson.

Baily, Heather (n.d.). "Posttraumatic Stress Disorder and Cultural Trauma." Senior thesis, anthropology, Colorado State University.

Barry, John M. (1997). *Rising Tide: The Great Mississippi Flood of 1927 and How It Changed America*. New York: Simon & Schuster.

Bates, David (2010). *The Katrina Paintings*. Knoxville, TN: Kemper Museum of Contemporary Art.

Bates, Kristin, and Richelle Swan (eds.) (2007). *Through the Eye of Katrina: Social Justice in the United States*. Durham, NC: Carolina Academic Press.

Bauder, David (2005). "Coverage of Katrina Bolsters Standing of Fox's Shepard Smith." *Seattle Times* (http://seattletimes.com/html/nationworld/2002520970 _katshep26.html).

Bechler, Brad (2009). *When Will the Sky Fall? Hurricane Katrina, a Documentary in Poetry*. Baltimore: Publish America.

Bellah, Robert (1991). *The Broken Covenant: American Civil Religion in Time of Trial*. Chicago: University of Chicago Press.

Berger, Dan (2009). "Constructing Crime, Framing Disaster: Routines of Criminalization and Crisis in Hurricane Katrina." *Punishment and Society* 11(4): 491–510.

Berry, John, Jonathan Foose, and Tad Jones (2009). *Up from the Cradle of Jazz: New Orleans Music since World War II*. Lafayette: University of Louisiana at Lafayette Press.

Biguenet, John, Steven Maklansky, and Tony Lewis (eds.) (2010). *Before (During) After: Louisiana Photographers' Visual Reactions to Hurricane Katrina*. New Orleans: University of New Orleans Press.

Boyd-Franklin, Nancy (2010). "Racism, Trauma and Resilience." In Wailoo et al.

Brinkley, Douglas (2006). *The Great Deluge: Hurricane Katrina, New Orleans, and the Mississippi Gulf Coast*. New York: Harper.

Breunlin, Rachel, and Helen Regis (2006). "Putting the Ninth Ward on the Map: Race, Place, and Transformation in Desire, New Orleans." *American Anthropologist* 108(4): 744–764.

Browne, Kate (2008). "From the Filmmaker, Still Waiting: Life after Katrina." *National Women's Studies Association Journal* 20(3): 196–199.

Bruni, Frank (2013). "Democrats Behaving Badly." *New York Times* Week in Review, January 13: 3.

Brunsma, David, David Overfelt, and Steven Pico (eds.) (2007). *The Sociology of Katrina: Perspectives on a Modern Catastrophe*. Lanham, MD: Rowman & Littlefield.

Burke, James Lee (2007). *The Tin Roof Blowdown*. New York: Pocket Books.

Bush, George (2010). *Decision Points*. New York: Crown Publishers.

Caruth, Cathy (1996). *Unclaimed Experience: Trauma, Narrative, and History*. Baltimore: Johns Hopkins University Press.

CNN Reports: Hurricane Katrina (2005). Kansas City: Andrews McMeel Publishing.

Cooper, Anderson (2010). *Dispatches from the Edge: A Memoir of War, Disasters and Survival*. New York: HarperCollins.

Czaja, Erica (2008). "Katrina's Southern 'Exposure': The Kanye Race Debate and the Repercussions of Discussion." In Marable and Clarke-Avery.

Chan, Paul (ed.) (2010). *Waiting for Godot in New Orleans: A Field Guide*. New York: Creative Time.

Cohn, Nik (2007). *Triksta: Life and Death and New Orleans Rap*. New York: Vintage Books.

David, Emmanuel (2008). "Cultural Trauma, Memory, and Gendered Collective Action: The Case of Women of the Storm Following Hurricane Katrina." *NWSA Journal* 20(3): 138–162.

David, Emmanuel, and Elaine Enarson (eds.) (2012). *The Women of Katrina: How Gender, Race, and Class Matter in an American Disaster*. Nashville: Vanderbilt University Press.

Davis, Elizabeth, and Kelly Rouba (2012). "Out of Sight, Out of Mind." In David and Enarson.

Daynes, Russell, and Havidan Rodriguez (2007). "Finding and Framing Katrina: The Social Construction of Disaster." In Brunsma et al.

Degloma, Thomas (2009). "Expanding Trauma through Space and Time: Mapping the Rhetorical Strategies of Trauma Carrier Groups." *Social Psychology Quarterly* 72: 105–122.

Department of Homeland Security (2006). *The Federal Response to Hurricane Katrina*. Washington, DC: Government Printing Office.

Dyson, Michael (2005). *Come Hell or High Water: Hurricane Katrina and the Color of Disaster*. New York: Basic Books.

Eggers, Dave (2009). *Zeitoun*. New York: Vintage.

Enarson, Elaine (2012). "Women and Girls Last." In David and Enarson.

Erikson, Kai (1994). *A New Species of Trouble: Explorations in Disaster, Trauma, and Community*. New York: W. W. Norton.

Erikson, Kai, and Lori Peek (2011). "Hurricane Katrina Research Bibliography." Social Science Research Council.

Eyerman, Ron (2008). *The Assassination of Theo van Gogh: From Social Drama to Cultural Trauma*. Durham, NC: Duke University Press.

Eyerman, Ron (2011). *The Cultural Sociology of Political Assassination: From MLK and RFK to Fortuyn and Van Gogh*. New York: Palgrave Macmillan.

Flynn, Stephen (2005). *America the Vulnerable: How Our Government Is Failing to Protect Us from Terrorism*. New York: Harper Perennial.

Ford, Kristina (2010). *The Trouble with City Planning: What New Orleans Can Teach Us*. New Haven, CT: Yale University Press.

Frailing, Kelly, and Dee Wood Harper (2007). "Crime and Hurricanes in New Orleans." In Brunsma et al.

Fuqua, Joy (2010). "The Big Apple and the Big Easy: Trauma, Proximity, and Home" in *Old and New Media after Katrina*. In Negra.

Fussell, Elizabeth (2007). "Constructing New Orleans, Constructing Race: A Population History of New Orleans." *Journal of American History* 94(3): 846–855.

Gordon, Ruth (2009). "Katrina, Race, Refugees, and Images of the Third World." In Levitt and Whitaker.

Gray, Peter, and Kendrick Oliver (eds.) (2004). *The Memory of Catastrophe*. Manchester, UK: Manchester University Press.

Greenberg, Michael (2013). "Occupy the Rockaways!" *New York Review of Books* 60(1) (January 10).

Greenlea, Stephanie (2014). "'Free the Jena 6': Racism and the Circuitry of Black Solidarity in the Digital." PhD diss., Yale University.

Groen, Jeffrey, and Anne Polivka (2009). "Going Home after Katrina: Determinants of Return Migration and Changes in Affected Areas." Working Paper 428, BLS Working Papers, U.S. Department of Labor.

Hall, Stuart (1980). "Encoding/Decoding." In *Culture, Media, Language*, ed. Stuart Hall et al. London: Hutchinson.

Haney, Timothy, et al. (2007). "Families and Hurricane Response: Evacuation, Separation, and Emotional Toll of Hurricane Katrina." In Brunsma et al.

Hanshaw, Sharon (2012). "Coastal Woman for Change." In David and Enarson.

Harris, Paul (2008). *Diary from the Dome: Reflections on Fear and Privilege during Katrina*. New York: Vantage.

Hartman, Chester, and Gregory Squires (eds.) (2006). *There Is No Such Thing as a Natural Disaster: Race, Class, and Hurricane Katrina*. New York: Routledge.

Horkheimer, Max, and Theodor Adorno. *Dialectic of Enlightenment*. New York: Herder and Herder.

Horne, Jed (2006). *Breach of Faith: Hurricane Katrina and the Near Death of a Great American City*. New York: Random House.

House of Representatives Committee on Government Reform (2005). *Back to the Drawing Board: A First Look at Lessons Learned from Katrina*. House of Representatives 109th Congress. Washington, DC: Government Printing Office.

Ignatieff, Michael (2005). "The Broken Contract." *New York Times*, September 25.

Kamel, Nabil (2012). "Social Marginalization, Federal Assistance and Repopulation Patterns in the New Orleans Metropolitan Area Following Hurricane Katrina." *Urban Studies* 49(14): 3211–3231.

Kaufman, Moisés, and the Members of the Tectonic Theater Project (2001). *The Laramie Project*. New York: Vintage Books.

Klein, Naomi (2005). "The Rise of Disaster Capitalism." *The Nation*, April 15.

LaCapra, Dominick (2001). *Writing History, Writing Trauma*. Baltimore: Johns Hopkins University Press.

Laska, Shirley (2008). "The 'Mother of All Rorschachs': Katrina Recovery in New Orleans." *Sociological Inquiry* 78(4): 580–591.

Lemann, Nicholas (1992). *The Promised Land: The Great Black Migration and How It Changed America*. New York: Vintage Books.

Lemann, Nicholas (2010). "Charm City, USA." *New York Review of Books*, September 30.

Lemann, Nicholas (2011). "The New New Orleans." *New York Review of Books*, March 24.

Levitt, Jeremy, and Matthew Whitaker (2009). *Hurricane Katrina: America's Unnatural Disaster*. Lincoln: University of Nebraska Press.

Little, Carl (2010). "Speaking Truth to Despair." In Bates.

Marable, Manning (2008). "Introduction." In Marable and Clarke-Avery.

Marable, Manning, and Kristen Clarke-Avery (eds.) (2008). *Seeking Higher Ground: The Hurricane Katrina Crisis, Race, and Public Policy Reader*. New York: Palgrave Macmillan.

Mayer, Aric (2008). "Aesthetics of Catastrophe." *Public Culture* 20(2): 177–191.

McQuaid, John, and Mark Schleifstein (2006). *Path of Destruction: The Devastation of New Orleans and the Coming Age of Superstorms*. New York: Little, Brown and Co.

Nagin, C. Ray (2010). *Katrina's Secrets*. Self-published.

Neal, Arthur (1998). *National Trauma and Collective Memory: Major Events in the American Century*. New York: M. E. Sharpe.

Negra, Diane (ed.) (2010). *Old and New Media after Katrina*. New York: Palgrave Macmillan.

Neiman, Susan (2005). *Evil in Modern Thought: An Alternative History of Philosophy*. Princeton, NJ: Princeton University Press.

Nelson, Marla, Renia Ehrenfeucht, and Shirley Laska (2007). "Planning, Plans, and People: Professional Expertise, Local Knowledge, and Governmental Action in Post-Katrina New Orleans." *Cityscape* 9(3): 23–52.

Neville, Charmaine (2007). "How We Survived the Flood." In South End Press Collective.

Olick, Jeffrey K. (2007). *The Politics of Regret: On Collective Memory and Historical Responsibility*. New York: Routledge.

Ostertag, Stephen, and David Ortiz (2013). "The Battle over Meaning: Digitally Mediated Processes of Cultural Trauma and Repair in the Wake of Hurricane Katrina." *American Journal of Cultural Sociology* 1(2): 186–220.

Peek, Lori (2010). *Behind the Backlash: Muslim Americans after 9/11*. Philadelphia: Temple University Press.

Peek, Lori, and Kai Erikson (2007). "Hurricane Katrina." In *Blackwell Encyclopedia of Sociology*, ed. George Ritzer. London: Blackwell Publishing.

Piazza, Tom (2005). *Why New Orleans Matters*. New York: Harper Collins.

Picou, Steven (2009). "Review Essay: The Shifting Sands of Post-Katrina Disaster Sociology." *Sociological Spectrum* 29: 431–438.

Polidori, Robert (2006). *After the Flood*. Göttingen: Steidi Publishers.

Potter, Hillary (ed.) (2007). *Racing the Storm: Racial Implications and Lessons Learned from Hurricane Katrina*. Lanham, MD: Lexington Books.

Potter, Hillary (2007). "Reframing Crime in a Disaster: Perception, Reality, and Criminalization of Survival Tactics among African Americans in the Aftermath of Katrina." In Potter.

Powell, Lawrence (2007). "What Does American History Tell Us about Katrina and Vice Versa?" *Journal of American History* 94(3): 863–876.

Powell, Lawrence (2012). *The Accidental City: Improvising New Orleans*. Cambridge, MA: Harvard University Press.

Quatentelli, E. L. (2005). "Catastrophes Are Different from Disasters: Some Implications for Crisis Planning and Managing Drawn from Katrina." http://under standingkatrina.ssrc.org/Quantelli/.

Quatentelli, E. L. (2006). "Notes on Antisocial and Criminal Behavior in Disasters, Catastrophes and Conflict Crises: The Research Evidence." Unpublished manuscript.

Raeburn, Bruce Boyd (2007). "'They're Tryin' to Wash Us Away': New Orleans Musicians Surviving Katrina." *Journal of American History* 94(3): 812–819.

Rebennack, Mac (Dr. John), with Jack Rummel (1994). *Under a Hoodoo Moon*. New York: St. Martin's Press.

Regis, Helen (2001). "Blackness and the Politics of Memory in the New Orleans Second Line." *American Ethnologist* 28(4): 752–777.

Regis, Helen, and Shana Walton (2008). "Producing the Folk at the New Orleans Jazz and Heritage Festival." *Journal of American Folklore* 121(482): 400–440.

Reid, Megan (2012). "Mothering after a Disaster." In David and Enarson.

Rich, Nathaniel (2012). "Jungleland." *New York Times Magazine*, March 25 (www .nytimes.com/2012/03/25/magazine/the-lower-ninth-ward-new-orleans.htm).

Rozario, Kevin (2007). *The Culture of Calamity: Disaster and the Making of Modern America*. Chicago: University of Chicago Press.

Rodriguez, Havidan, Joseph Trainor, and Enrico Quarantelli (2006). "Rising to the Challenge of a Catastrophe: The Emergent and Prosocial Behavior following Hurricane Katrina." *Annals of the American Academy of Political and Social Science* 604: 82–101.

Roahen, Sara (2008). *Gumbo Tales: Finding My Place at the New Orleans Table*. New York: W. W. Norton.

Rose, Chris (2007). *1 Dead in Attic: After Katrina*. New York: Simon & Schuster.

Rove, Karl (2010). *Courage and Consequence: My Life as a Conservative in the Fight*. New York: Threshold Editions.

Sandusky, Phil (2007). *Painting Katrina*. Gretna, LA: Pelican Publishing.

Seager, Joni (2012). "Noticing Gender (or Not) in Disasters." In David and Enarson.

Senate Committee on Health, Education, Labor, and Pensions (2005). *Examining Rebuilding Lives and Communities after Hurricane Katrina*. United States Senate 109th Congress. Washington, DC: Government Printing Office.

Sommers, Samuel, Evan Apfelbaum, Kristin Dukes, Negin Toosi, and Elsie Wang (2006). "Race and Media Coverage of Hurricane Katrina: Analysis, Implications, and Future Research Questions." *Analysis of Social Issues and Public Policy* 6(1): 39–55.

Sontag, Susan (2003). *Regarding the Pain of Others*. New York: Picador.

South End Press Collective (eds.) (2007). *What Lies Beneath*. Cambridge: South End Press.

Spera, Keith (2011). *Groove Interrupted: Loss, Renewal, and the Music of New Orleans*. New York: Picador.

Spielman, David (2007). *Katrinaville Chronicles: Images and Observations from a New Orleans Photographer*. Baton Rouge: Louisiana State University Press.

Steinberg, Ted (2000). *Acts of God: The Unnatural History of Natural Disaster in America*. New York: Oxford.

Swenson, John (2011). *New Atlantis: Musicians Battle for the Survival of New Orleans*. New York: Oxford.

Sylvester, Judith (2008). *The Media and Hurricanes Katrina and Rita: Lost and Found*. New York: Palgrave Macmillan.

Syzerhans, Douglas (ed.) (2006). *Federal Disaster Programs and Hurricane Katrina*. New York: Nova Science Publishers.

Tierney, Kathleen (2008). "Hurricane in New Orleans? Who Knew? Anticipating Katrina and Its Devastation." *Sociological Inquiry* 78(2): 179–183.

Tierney, Kathleen, Christine Benc, and Erica Kuligowski (2006). "Metaphors Matter: Disaster Myths, Media Frames and Their Consequences in Hurricane Katrina." *Annals of the American Academy of Political and Social Science* 604: 57–81.

Thevenot, Brian (2006). "Myth-Making in New Orleans." *American Journalism Review*, December/January.

Trauth, Suzanne, and Lisa Brenner (eds.) (2011). *Katrina on Stage: Five Plays*. Evanston, IL: Northwestern University Press.

Trethewey, Natasha (2010). *Beyond Katrina: A Meditation on the Mississippi Gulf Coast*. Athens: University of Georgia Press.

Tyler, Pamela (2007). "The Post-Katrina, Semiseparate World of Gender Politics." *Journal of American History* 94(3): 780–788.

Van Heerden, Ivor (2007). *The Storm: What Went Wrong and Why during Hurricane Katrina, the Inside Story from One Louisiana Scientist*. New York: Penguin Books.

Vannini, Philip, and Aaron McCright (2007). "Technologies of the Sky." *Critical Discourse Studies* 4(1): 49–73.

Wailoo, Keith, Karen O'Neill, Jeffrey Dowd, and Roland Anglin (eds.) (2010).

Katrina's Imprint: Race and Vulnerability in America. New Brunswick, NJ: Rutgers University Press.

Weber, Lynn, and Lori Peek (2012). *Displaced: Life in the Katrina Diaspora*. Austin: University of Texas Press.

Willinger, Beth, and Janna Knight (2012). "Setting the Stage for Disaster." In David and Enarson.

Zotti, Marianne, Van Tong, Lyn Kieltyka, and Renee Brown-Bryant (2012). "Factors Influencing Evacuation Decisions among High-Risk Pregnant and Postpartum Women." In David and Enarson.

Zunes, Stephen (2005). "Hurricane Katrina and the War in Iraq." www.commondreams.org.

ABOUT THE AUTHOR AND SERIES EDITOR

RON EYERMAN is a professor of sociology and codirector of the Center for Cultural Sociology at Yale University in New Haven, Connecticut. His previous books include *Cultural Trauma: Slavery and the Formation of African American Identity* and *Narrating Trauma: On the Impact of Collective Suffering.*

KAI ERIKSON, SERIES EDITOR, is Professor Emeritus of Sociology and American Studies at Yale University. He is a past president of the American Sociological Association, winner of the MacIver and Sorokin Awards from the ASA, and author of *A New Species of Trouble: Explorations in Disaster, Trauma, and Community*, and his research and teaching interests include American communities, human disasters, and ethnonational conflict.

INDEX

Adorno, Theodor, 17–18, 70, 73
Allen, Thad, 116
Alter, Jonathan, 42, 44–46, 125
American identity, 15, 42–44, 56, 123–125, 129–130, 145–147. *See also* American nation
American nation, 1–2, 8, 123–124, 126–127, 129, 130–131, 145–147. *See also* American identity
Amoss, Jim, 25, 32, 52
Armstrong, Louis, 88
Army Corps of Engineers, 33, 37, 85, 86, 88, 132, 142, 147

Barbour, Haley, 29, 108
Bates, David, 75–77
Beckett, Samuel, 87
Belcher, Brad, 82, 138
Bellah, Robert, 1
Berger, Peter, 11
Blanchard, Terence, 60–61, 76, 87–88, 139
Blanchard, Wilhelmina, 60–61, 139
Blanco, Kathleen, 3, 30, 87, 98, 101, 113, 117, 134
Boudreaux, Monk, 56
Brecht, Bertolt, 86
Brenner, Lisa, 86
Brinkley, Douglas, 3
Broussard, Aaron, 108
Brown, Aaron, 97–99, 104–107, 110, 111–112, 114, 115–116, 137
Brown, Michael, 3, 22, 48, 69, 87, 101, 111, 113, 115–116, 117, 122, 134
Bruni, Frank, 143
Burke, Edmund, 72
Burke, James Lee, 85
Burnett, John, 150n2
Bush, George H. W., 15
Bush, George W., 3, 11, 14, 17, 23, 29–30, 34, 37, 43, 44, 45, 48–49, 65–66, 69, 97–98, 100–104, 107, 111, 113, 115, 124, 132, 133, 134–135
Bush, Laura, 15

carrier groups, 9, 15–16, 21–22, 40, 131–133, 146
Caruth, Cathy, 40, 137
Chan, Paul, 87
Charles, Ray, 65
Chertoff, Michael, 22, 100, 107, 108, 111, 113, 116, 117, 134
City That Care Forgot, 68–69
civil religion, 1–2
Clarke, Lee, 39–40
class, 5, 25, 27, 50, 116, 119, 124. *See also under* race
Clinton, Bill, 97
CNN (Cable News Network), 16, 24, 69, 87, 96–99, 100–102, 104–107, 108–119
collective identity, 6, 7–8, 10–11, 15, 40–41, 62–63, 65, 71, 129–131, 146; and individual identity, 129
collective memory, 15, 130, 141–145, 146–147
Collins, Susan, 114
commercial interests: tension with aesthetic concerns, 18–19, 70, 74–75, 84; tension with news reportage, 116–117
Compass, Eddie, III, 103
Convention Center, 12, 22, 32, 33, 39, 97, 104, 106, 109, 110, 112, 136
Cooke, Sam, 116
Cooper, Anderson, 96–97, 110, 111–112, 117–118, 137, 138
covenant, sacred, 1–4, 7, 15, 27, 50–51, 56, 123–124, 130–131, 149n1
cultural trauma, 6–19, 39, 40–41, 51, 110, 120, 130–131, 140, 145–146

DeLay, Tom, 111, 115
DeParle, Jason, 36

Department of Homeland Security, 3, 15, 22, 48, 114–115, 134–135, 141–142
Dobbs, Lou, 101
documentary realism, 72–73, 87–88
Domino, Fats, 58, 65
Dowd, Maureen, 38–39
Dr. John (Mac Rebennack), 56, 63–64, 68–70
Duchamp, Marcel, 85
Dylan, Bob, 59
Dyson, Michael, 13

emotion, 9–10, 40–41, 60–64, 74–77, 82–83, 85–86, 108–110, 116, 131, 138–140
empathy, 41, 43–44, 70, 72–74, 96, 109–110, 129, 138, 140, 146
Erikson, Kai, 6–7, 9, 39–41
Evans, Walter, 76
experts, 41, 132

Farrakhan, Louis, 11
Fats Domino. See Domino, Fats
FEMA (Federal Emergency Management Agency), 3, 15, 21–22, 34, 48, 110, 113, 117, 122, 134, 143, 147
film, 16, 18, 26, 53, 60–61, 87–89, 143–144
flag, American, 98–99
Floodwall (Napoli), 79–80
Flynn, Stephen, 114
free will, 126–127
French, Dyan (Mamma D), 5
Freud, Sigmund, 40, 137
Fuqua, Joy, 80

"Georgia Bush," (Lil Wayne), 65–67
Gergen, David, 111
Giuliani, Rudy, 134, 142
Gould, Alan, 104
Gray, Terius (Juvenile), 58, 65
Greenberg, Michael, 125
Greenfield, Jeff, 114
Gupta, Sanjay, 105

Haberdasher, M. D., 74
Hall, Stuart, 49

Hannity, Sean, 136
Harrington, Michael, 1, 44–45, 125
Hays, Aimee, 86
heroes, 28–31, 55, 80, 122, 134, 135, 146
Holcombe, David, 77
Honoré, Russel, 103, 106, 134, 141
Horisaki, Takashi, 78–79, 81
Horkheimer, Max, 73
Huffington, Arianna, 125
Hurricane Andrew, 48, 61, 93
Hurricane Betsy, 5
Hurricane Camille, 5, 93
Hurricane Irene, 92
Hurricane Katrina: aesthetic response to, 17–18, 52–91; assigning blame for, 110–116, 123–124, 140–141; as chaos and crisis story, 95–99, 123; comparisons to 9/11, 68, 80, 93–94, 99, 111, 113–116, 141–142, 146–147; comparisons to other hurricanes, 4–5; as cultural trauma, 12–19; effects on African Americans, 13–16, 67, 127–130, 132–133, 145–146; effects on elderly, 25, 71, 145–146; as event, 13–14, 15–16, 49, 121–123; governmental response to, 2–4, 37–38, 100–116, 123, 133–135; as human interest story, 94–95; naming and coding of, 4–6, 121; as "national shame," 14, 39, 43, 44, 80, 127, 130, 146; as natural disaster, 29, 33, 77, 122, 131, 140; political context of, 133–135; print media representations of, 23–51; as recovery/repair/rescue story, 26, 31–37, 107–110; religious interpretations of, 11–12, 131; representational issues of, 17–18, 54–56, 91, 135–141; responsibility for, 46–48, 66, 126; and shift in narrative from natural to social disaster, 37–40; as social disaster, 33, 77, 122, 131–133, 135, 140, 146; as storm story, 20, 26, 135, 92–94, 135; struggle over meaning of, 131–133; as survival story, 20, 31–35, 37, 50, 84, 126; televised representations of, 92–119; as war zone, 29–30, 34, 39, 46, 99, 103–104, 135
Hurricane Sandy, 125, 142–143

identity. *See* American identity; collective identity

ideology, 126–129

Ignatieff, Michael, 149n1

Internet, 16–17, 20, 66–68, 79, 87, 128

interpretation, 9, 70–72, 121

Johnson, Lyndon, 1–2, 44, 56

journalists, 8–9, 41, 49, 117, 135–137, 145

Jencks, Christopher, 36

Juvenile (Terius Gray), 58, 65

Kant, Immanuel, 72–73

Katrina. *See* Hurricane Katrina

Katrina and Beyond, 54–56

"Katrina Klap" ("Dollar Day"), 18, 67, 69

Kennedy, John F., 15

King, Larry, 104

King, Martin Luther, Jr., 15

Klein, Joe, 46–47

Kroll-Smith, Steve, 39, 125–126

Kubrick, Stanley, 88

LaCapra, Dominik, 138

LaGrone, Libra, 59

Landrieu, Mary, 96–97

Landrieu, Mitch, 112

Lange, Dorothea, 76

Lawrence, Chris, 97

Lee, Spike, 14, 16, 18, 60, 87–91, 139–140

Lefemine, Steve, 11

Leibniz, Gottfried, 11

Lemann, Nicholas, 89

Lewis, Jerry, 104

Lewis, John, 42–43, 125

Liberator, Grace, 77

Lil Wayne (Dwayne Michael Carter, Jr.), 14, 17, 18, 58, 65–71, 133, 152n30; "Georgia Bush," 65–67

Lincoln, Abraham, 1

looting/lawlessness, media representations of, 26–28, 30–31, 32, 35–36, 38–39, 46, 84, 94–95, 97–99, 115

Maestri, Walter, 93

Mangano, Mabel, 77

Mangano, Salvador, 77

mass media, 9–10, 15–17, 20–22, 40–41, 49–51, 87, 100, 106, 110, 116, 123–124, 126, 132, 135–137, 140–141, 144–146; tension between local and national, 21–28

Matthews, Chris, 100

Mattingly, David, 97–98

Mayer, Aric, 20, 72

McLuhan, Marshall, 150n15

McQuaid, John, 37, 53, 150n24

meaning, 6–19, 31, 40–42, 50, 60–62, 65, 70–71, 81, 120–123, 129–133

memory, 5, 66–67, 80–82, 93–94, 110, 121, 138. *See also* collective memory

Mill, John Stuart, 127

Mos Def (Yasiin Bey), 14, 17, 18, 65, 67–70, 133

music, 18, 56–72, 86, 88, 90, 139–140, 152n12, 152n27; and context, 60–64; generational aspects of, 65; genre aspects of, 65–70; as politicized, 57, 65–71

Nagin, Ray, 3, 4, 11, 17, 22, 23, 30, 35, 77, 86–87, 95, 96, 100–101, 103, 104, 105, 108, 113, 117, 122, 127, 134, 140, 142

Napoli, Jana, 79–80, 81

narrative frames, 8, 10, 49, 121, 122, 135–137, 145

narratives, 6, 8–12, 15–16, 26, 37, 40, 93–94, 119, 121–123, 126. *See also* narrative frames

nation. *See* American nation

NBC (National Broadcasting Company), 16, 94–96, 99, 100, 102–104, 107–108, 110, 113, 115–119

Neal, Arthur, 8–9

Negra, Diane, 53, 81

Neiman, Susan, 12

Neville, Aaron, 62, 116

Neville, Cyril, 56

Newman, Andy, 142

New Orleans: music of, 57–59, 64, 71–72; neighborhoods of, 57–59, 71–72; representations of, 52–54, 122; as "third-world" setting, 40, 42, 45, 104, 105

Newsweek, 16, 39, 42–46

New York Times, 16, 23–24, 29–31, 33, 35–40, 49, 66

Obama, Barack, 15, 133
Osborne, Terrance, 18, 74, 139
Overmyer, Eric, 90

painting, 70, 73–79, 138–139
Pelosi, Nancy, 111, 115
perpetrators, 10, 28–31, 55–56, 69, 131, 135, 145–146. *See also* villains
personalization of, 29–30
photography, 17, 70, 72–74, 82–85, 110, 116–117, 138, 144; vs. painting, 76–77, 83; in print media, 23–49
poetry, 17, 70, 81–82, 85–86, 138
police department, New Orleans, 3, 83–84; media representations of, 26–28, 32, 39, 95, 97, 98–99, 104–105
Porche West, Christopher, 78
Porter, George, 56
poverty, 13, 44–45, 116, 125, 128, 145–146. *See also under* race
Pryor, Mark, 3

race, 5, 12–16, 25, 27–28, 30, 32, 43–44, 50, 66–68, 71–72, 95, 100, 116, 119, 124; and class, 10–11, 12–13, 34, 105–106, 124, 125–129; and poverty, 21, 36–37, 80, 106, 124, 132–133, 143–144, 145–146
racism, 1, 14, 15, 40, 127–129
Raeburn, Bruce Boyd, 152n27
Reid, Harry, 143
Relle, Frank, 83
Rice, Condoleezza, 107
Ripley, Amanda, 46–47
Rivera, Geraldo, 136
Robertson, Pat, 11
Rose, Chris, 60, 68
Rosen, Jody, 66
Rousseau, Jean-Jacques, 11–12, 29, 47
Rumsfeld, Donald, 107
Russert, Tim, 108

Saffir-Simpson Scale, 4, 93, 121
Sanchez, Paul, 61–62
Sandusky, Phil, 74–77, 82–83, 139

Savage, Martin, 94, 96
Schleifstein, Mark, 23, 37, 150n24
Seigenthaler, John, 99
Shepard, Matthew, 86
Shetterley, Robert, 76
shocking incident. *See* traumatic occurrence
Simon, David, 90
Simons, Dona, 77
Smelser, Neil, 9, 39
Smith, Bessie, 62
Smith, Shepard, 136, 137, 138
sociology, 41, 125–129, 145
Sontag, Susan, 70, 72–73, 144
Spera, Keith, 61
Spielman, David, 83–84
Springsteen, Bruce, 59, 62, 65
Superdome, 7, 12, 23, 24, 25–26, 30, 31–32, 33, 46, 55, 63, 94–95, 101, 107, 122–123, 124, 145
Swenson, John, 59, 61, 71–72

television, 26, 49–50, 92–119, 137, 138–140; as building imagined community, 104; as "cool" medium, 26, 109, 138; public service role of, 108–110
theater, 85–87
Thomas, Irma, 62
Time, 45–49
Times-Picayune, New Orleans, 16, 23–28, 31–37, 49, 107, 144–145
trauma: collective traumatic occurrence, 6–11, 14, 17, 18, 39–41, 60–63, 80, 113, 140–141; individual, 7, 17, 18, 39–41, 60–63, 80, 113; levels of, 6–8, 17, 18; narration of, 8–12; national, 8–9, 14, 80, 146–147; representation of, 137–141. *See also* cultural trauma
traumatic occurrence, 6–8, 18, 40–41, 53, 62–63, 64, 70
Trauth, Suzanne, 86
Treme, 89–91
Trethewey, Natasha, 81–82
Tubbs Jones, Stephanie, 105–106

Varisco, Tom, 77–78
victims, 10–11, 14–15, 17–18, 28–31, 32,

35–37, 46–47, 50, 55–56, 69, 73, 80, 92, 96, 119, 122, 127–130, 131, 135, 140–141, 145–146; personalization of, 29–30, 96; represented as refugees, 29–30, 40, 96, 102, 104, 119, 129–130, 144

villains, 28–31, 32, 35–36, 55, 80, 122, 135, 146. *See also* perpetrators

visual arts, 72–82, 138–139; and context, 84–85; as political, 77–78. *See also* painting; photography

Voices of the Wetlands, 56–57, 58

Voltaire (François-Marie Arouet), 11–12, 29, 47

Warhol, Andy, 85

Weber, Max, 11

West, Kanye, 14, 133

When the Levees Broke (Lee), 60, 87–89, 139–140

Whitaker, Mark, 44

White, Dr. Michael, 63–64

Will, George, 38

Williams, Brian, 94–96, 102–103, 110–111, 115–116, 117–118, 138

Williams, Tennessee, 101

Wood, James, 12